Response Guides
for Teaching Children's Books

Response Guides
for Teaching Children's Books

Albert B. Somers
Furman University

Janet Evans Worthington
West Virginia Institute of Technology

National Council of Teachers of English
1111 Kenyon Road, Urbana, Illinois 61801

NCTE Editorial Board: Evelyn M. Copeland, Rudine Sims, Donald C. Stewart, Ann Terry, Frank Zidonis, Robert F. Hogan, *ex officio*, Paul O'Dea, *ex officio*.

Book Design: Tom Kovacs.

NCTE Stock Number: 40866.

Library of Congress Cataloging in Publication Data

Somers, Albert B   1939–
  Response guides for teaching children's books.

  1. Children's literature–Study and teaching.
2. Books and reading for children.
I. Worthington, Janet Evans, 1942–   joint
author. II. Title.
LB 1575.S56   372.6'4   79–18
ISBN 0-8141-4086-6

Contents

Introduction:
Building Fires about Books

In Chapter 7 of Robert Lawson's *Rabbit Hill*, one of the workmen hired to rebuild the stone wall near the Big House attributes the New Folks' unusual liking of small animals to their reading of books: "Makes 'em queer, that's what it does. . . . Grandpa had the right of it. 'Readin' rots the mind,' *he* used to say."[1] Although Tim McGrath can hardly be considered the typical American, his attitude toward reading and books is not uncommon among American youth and adults. Many of us reject reading; we either cannot read well or do not like to read or both. It is a national problem.

Obviously the problem can be overstated. Most of us cope well enough with print; we read signs, soup cans, tax notices, Dear Abby, menus, the sports page, and Harold Robbins. But relatively few of us read for joy and insight as well as for pleasure and profit; few of us enrich our lives with reading.

Unfortunately and unfairly, the blame for any reading problem is always placed on the American schools. The schools, it is so simply argued, do not teach us how to read. The truth, however, is that the schools are reasonably successful in teaching Americans the fundamental skills of reading. Despite inevitable failures, they turn out hordes of students every year who can easily read their way through the Yellow Pages and the *National Inquirer*. What the schools too often fail to do, we argue, is to excite children about reading. They present no convincing case for reading as a lifelong habit that is pleasurable, meaningful, enlightening, and rewarding. They fail to build fires about books.

The reasons for this failure of the American schools are so numerous and complicated that they defy easy analysis. Administrative and parental apathy, lack of classroom time, large classes, inadequate budgets, censorship, television, and a host of other causes all play a part. Another contributing factor, we believe, is American education's love affair with the basal reader as the *sine qua non* of reading instruction and the subsequent neglect of children's books as a valid cornerstone of any reading program.

---

[1] Robert Lawson, *Rabbit Hill* (New York: Viking Press, 1944), pp. 82, 84.

The neglect of children's books in the elementary school classroom is deceptive: after all, books *are* read to children, elementary school libraries *are* more numerous than ever, and book clubs *do* flourish in many schools. Still, in most schools, children's literature is not at the forefront of the reading program, but rather somewhere off to the side—like Crow Boy in Taro Yashima's book. The neglect has several causes, three of which stand out. (1) Literature, along with art and music, is often out of favor with the American public and is considered by many to be, at best, a frill. (2) There is little room for children's books what with all the time spent on the basal reader in the morning, math in the afternoon, and the rest of the basics in between. (3) Many teachers—including those who thoroughly enjoy children's literature—lack the time or training to promote books by designing the learning experiences that emphasizing them would require. We will respond to these three sources of neglect with the following contentions.

(1) No educational program of quality in this country can afford to ignore the contributions that literature can make to the well-being of its children. In addition to providing motivation and inspiration, literature offers children more opportunities than any other area of the curriculum to consider ideas, values, and ethical questions crucial to our development as moral human beings. In what better way, for example, can a teacher encourage empathy for the downtrodden and respect for courage than by leading a class through *Sounder*?

(2) Rather than demanding more from an already cramped classroom schedule, children's books can blend effectively into present programs by serving as the means of interrelating not only the language arts but also other areas of the curriculum. The reading of *Where the Wild Things Are* in the first grade and *Old Yeller* in the sixth can generate a variety of art, drama, and composing activities. Books of a caliber similar to *The Matchlock Gun* and *A Wrinkle in Time* are often firmly grounded in history or science.

(3) We consider valid the claim by many teachers that they lack the time to design effective and exciting learning experiences around children's books. Teachers frequently read books like *Charlotte's Web* and *The Borrowers* to children, but they seldom use the books as sources of activities and instruction. For many it is difficult just to find the time to *read* the books, much less prepare an array of questions and activities that will effectively involve children in and beyond the books. It is largely for these teachers that this volume has been written.

The purpose of *Response Guides for Teaching Children's Books*, then, is to provide teachers with guides that will help them light small fires with books, kindling an enthusiasm for reading while at the same time reinforcing the teaching of reading skills and inter-relating the language arts with other areas of the curriculum. Guides to twenty-seven works of children's fiction are included, arranged in order of increasing difficulty. There are ten picture books, four "transitional" novels (*The Hundred Penny Box, The Courage of Sarah Noble, The Matchlock Gun,* and *Rabbit Hill*), and thirteen longer novels. The selection of these titles has been based on answers to two main questions—Is the book of high quality? Is it popular with children?—and several secondary questions—Is the book teachable? Does it have significant themes? Does the total selection offer a balance between realism and fantasy? Will both boys and girls enjoy the book? Are minorities treated fairly and honestly in the book? Obviously many excellent, popular books have been omitted; any teacher could easily supply a list of his or her favorites that are not included. We hope, however, that these twenty-seven response guides will serve as starting points, suggesting experiences that could be used, with modification, to help children respond to other books as teachers find time to de-velop their own activities and questions.

Our selection of the term *response guide* is intentional. It is important that teachers recognize that each of the twenty-seven units has been planned to serve only as a guide, consisting of *sug-gested* activities and questions, experiences that a teacher may use or disregard as determined by the needs, abilities, interests, and concerns of the class or group reading the book. In designing the experiences, we have tried to focus on *response*, on the active, participative interaction of children with these books, in such a way as to promote insight and enthusiasm. These are not, there-fore, study guides. Though teachers may choose at times to give quizzes as reading checks, no test questions per se are provided in this book.

All twenty-seven response guides follow the same format. Each opens with a brief plot *Summary* sketching the highlights of the narrative. Included here is a list of the *Themes* the book empha-sizes. These central ideas are important, for they serve as the focus of many activities and discussion questions. The list should not be considered complete, however; teachers may identify and empha-size themes that we have overlooked. Next, a brief *Appraisal* dis-cusses the book's possible appeal to children, its particular strengths, and perhaps information relevant to its origin and reputation.

The section entitled *Reading Considerations* focuses on the problems children may have in reading that particular book. Comments include appropriate references to plot, sentence structure, and especially vocabulary. The vocabulary lists included in this section are selective, with each word included on the basis of its significance in the book (that is, the extent to which the word is important to comprehension of a significant passage), the frequency with which the word appears, and the probability of its being assimilated into the vocabulary of children who would most likely read the book.[2] A teacher might introduce some of the words briefly prior to reading or ignore them if he or she prefers. We do not encourage teachers to use children's books primarily as a source of words for vocabulary study.

Experiences that will precede the reading of the book are provided in the *Initiating Activities* section. They suggest ways for the teacher to introduce children to the book; they set the stage. An initiating activity will often direct the children's attention to one of the book's major conflicts or themes by asking individuals or small groups to discuss certain questions, act out a structured situation, or participate in some other activity that encourages them to anticipate the book.

The purpose of the *Discussion Questions* is to promote a variety of thoughtful responses to the book. Some of the questions require that the student merely recall a detail or incident (as in the question "How does Max get to 'where the wild things are'?"). Others encourage different kinds of thinking: (a) convergent questions that require the child to infer and synthesize ("Why is Max smiling when he gets back to his room?"); (b) divergent questions that require the reader to think beyond the book and perhaps within his or her own self ("What would you have done with the wild things?"); and (c) evaluative questions that require the reader to make judgments ("Was it fair to send Max to bed without his supper?"). Here we hasten to encourage teachers to select only questions they wish to ask; in the primary grades especially, this selection might include just two or three questions for a given book.[3]

The last sections of each guide suggest various activities in *Art and Media, Creative Dramatics,* and *Composing.* In each area we

---

[2] Teachers should note that page numbers in the word lists and elsewhere in the guides refer to the hardback edition of a book. The paperback pagination may differ.

[3] Those questions designed specifically to further literary awareness by encouraging the perceptive appreciation of a book's theme, character development, plot, and so on are indicated throughout by asterisks.

have tried to provide experiences that are enjoyable, worthwhile in their provision of opportunities to practice skills, and significant in the context of the book's themes and values. Our intent has been to design activities that will excite children to the potential that books offer and encourage them to make enlightened judgments about characters and themes.

Finally, at the end of each guide is a list of *Instructional Resources*, which includes audiovisual materials, articles, and teaching guides appropriate for use with the book.[4]

We hope that this book and the individual response guides that comprise it will find multiple uses. Implementation will surely vary as much as do the teachers who discover the book: some may select an activity or two here and there, while others may consider each guide a lesson plan. We offer but a few suggestions.

(1) We hope that teachers who select a particular guide for use will read the book for which that guide is intended. In the upper grades of the elementary school at least, it would be possible for a teacher to provide small groups of children with questions and activities without having read the book, but this approach is not recommended. Children often have questions about a book that only an adult who has read the book can answer.

(2) We insist that teachers modify the activities and questions as necessary to meet the specific needs and abilities of their students. Invariably, for given groups or classes, some of the suggested activities and questions will be too difficult or complicated; some may be too easy. Some will refer to materials that are not available or to techniques that are not familiar. However, we believe most of them can be used, with possible minor alterations, often with exciting and rewarding results.

(3) At times the suggested experiences may simply be too few in number, a possible inadequacy that leads to our third suggestion: teachers should supplement our activities and questions with their own. Our experience is that most elementary school teachers are long on creativity in the development of activities, but short on the time to be creative. The response guides in this book should provide a foundation upon which teachers can design additional experiences for children as time allows.

(4) Although the guides can be used in any kind of classroom format from traditional to open, many of the suggested experiences, especially with the longer books, imply (or require) small-group work in which children share and interact with each other.

---

[4] Addresses of companies referred to in this section are listed in the Appendix.

(In fact, because we feel older children should be encouraged to work directly from the guides, the activities for the thirteen longer books are directed to the students rather than the teacher, although the teacher will organize and manage the overall learning experience directly or indirectly.) Our suggestion, then, is that teachers in the upper grades should often allow students the freedom and the responsibility of working in small groups—discussing characters, acting out improvisations, sharing reports—in an effort to promote greater understanding and appreciation of these books.

How are books like these twenty-seven presented to children? In the primary grades, of course, they are most frequently read aloud. At the intermediate level many are read aloud (surely *Charlotte's Web*, for one) while others are experienced in small groups in which children read their own copies of the book. It really doesn't matter. What matters is that children read or listen to the books and then have many opportunities to get involved in them so that any sparks of excitement they give off in response to good books can be fanned into fires of warm enthusiasm toward reading as a meaningful lifelong habit.

We hope this small book will help kindle the flame.

Acknowledgments

We would like to acknowledge the encouragement and assistance of family and friends in the writing of this book, especially of Rachael (age 11), Susannah (age 10), and Evan (age 8), all of whom reinforced our feelings about the books and occasionally stayed out of our way. Also, though the guides are our responsibility, we are grateful to students and teachers we have known who responded favorably to the idea behind the book and encouraged its completion.

Albert B. Somers
Janet Evans Worthington

Where the Wild Things Are

By Maurice Sendak. (New York: Harper & Row, Publishers, 1963. Available in paperback from Scholastic Book Services.)

Summary

Sent to bed without his supper, Max imagines a trip to a place inhabited by various wild things. Despite their ferociousness, Max tames them by staring into their eyes without blinking and leads them in a wild rumpus. Feeling lonely, he finally leaves the protesting creatures and sails back to his own room, where a warm supper is waiting. Themes: security, the child in control of a threatening situation.

Appraisal

This is surely one of the most popular of all picture books, written by an exceptionally able and creative author-illustrator. The book is wild, engaging, and thoroughly satisfying to primary grade children. It won the Caldecott Medal in 1964.

Reading Considerations

Where the Wild Things Are is simple in plot, but the vocabulary (*mischief, gnashed, private, terrible,* and *rumpus*) and sentences that stretch over several pages require that it be read aloud, at least to most primary grade children.

Initiating Activities

1. Show the children the third of the large double-page spreads in the middle of the book (where Max is riding one of the wild things). Ask them what they think is happening and what the book is about.

7

   2. Let children talk about monsters such as the Cookie Monster and King Kong for several minutes.

Discussion Questions

   1. Why is Max sent to bed without supper? Do you think this is fair? Has this ever happened to you? How did you feel?
   2. What grows in Max's room that night? Would you like this to happen in your room? Does Max like it? How can you tell? What would you do if you woke up one morning and your room was filled with trees, bushes, and vines?
   3. How does Max get to where the wild things are? Is it possible to sail "through night and day and in and out of weeks and almost over a year"? How?
   4. What do the wild things look like? Which one do you think looks the wildest? Why? Which one looks partly like a person? In what way?
  *5. How does Max feel when he first meets the wild things? How can you be sure?
   6. What does Max do to the wild things? What do you think you would have done? Why do the wild things make him their king?
   7. Why does Max finally decide he wants to leave?
  *8. How does Max feel when he returns home? How can you tell? Why do you suppose he feels this way?

Art and Media

   1. Let children draw their own pictures—perhaps a mural or frieze—of wild things. Do not limit them to the kinds of creatures found in the book.
   2. As the story is acted out (see Creative Dramatics #3), have an older child take pictures with a Polaroid camera. Then have the children arrange the pictures in the proper sequence for a box movie.

Creative Dramatics

   1. Let children dance the wild rumpus to rhythmic accompaniment or perhaps to music (such as a recording of "The Baby Elephant's Walk" by Henry Mancini).

2. Have the children act out a conversation between Max and his mother after he returns to his room.
3. Let four or five children act out the whole story.

Composing

1. Let a child (or several) record or dictate a story about (a) their favorite one of the wild things, or (b) the wild thing that has human feet.
2. Have children write a note that Max might have left for his mother before leaving or one that he might have sent later.

Instructional Resources

Record—*Where the Wild Things Are*, Weston Woods (LTR 84), 33 rpm, $1.95.
Cassette—*Where the Wild Things Are*, Weston Woods (LTR 84C), $5.50.
Filmstrip—*Where the Wild Things Are*, Weston Woods, $7.25 for filmstrip only (FS 84), $9.20 with record (SF 84), $12.75 with cassette (SF 84C).
Film—*Where the Wild Things Are*, Weston Woods, 8 minutes, animated, color; $150.00 (sale), $10.00 (rental).
Poster—*Where the Wild Things Are*, Scholastic (#6072), 29″ by 41″, $1.50.
Teaching Guide—Charlotte S. Huck, *Children's Literature in the Elementary School*, 3rd ed. (New York: Holt, Rinehart and Winston, 1976), pp. 729-30.
Teaching Guide—"Where the Wild Things Are," *A Curriculum for English, Grade 1* (Lincoln: University of Nebraska Press, 1966).

The Tale of Peter Rabbit

By Beatrix Potter. (New York: Frederick Warne and Co., 1901, 59 pp. Available in paperback from Scholastic Book Services and Dover Publications.)

Summary

Peter Rabbit, a naughty bunny, invades Mr. McGregor's garden, despite his mother's warnings. He is chased by the farmer, and after several narrow escapes he finds his way out of the garden. When he returns home, he is confined to bed. Themes: responsibility, the importance of obeying parents.

Appraisal

Beatrix Potter's classic tale has been a favorite with generations of children who have recognized their own world in the lives of her animal characters. The illustrations in gentle pastels help to make the miniature volume popular with children from two to eight.

Reading Considerations

Although the plot and sentence structure of this story present few problems, its vocabulary may. Important words include *mischief*, *naughty*, *implored*, *exert*, *sieve*, and *fortnight*.

Initiating Activities

1. Explain to the children that sometimes the things we are told not to do seem so very inviting and exciting. Ask if they have ever done anything they were told definitely not to do. What happened to them?

2. Have children make up a story in which a small person or animal is chased by a giant figure of some kind. Each child adds a sentence in sequence.

Discussion Questions

1. Why doesn't Mrs. Rabbit want her children to go into Mr. McGregor's garden? How do you think Mr. Rabbit might have been caught? Why do you suppose Peter disobeys his mother? Should Mrs. Rabbit have left the children by themselves?
2. What does Peter do when he finds out he is lost? Have you ever been lost? What did you do? What is the smartest thing to do if you are lost?
3. Why do you think the sparrows help Peter escape?
4. Why does Peter hide in the can? Why is it a good hiding place? Why isn't it a good hiding place?
*5. Why doesn't Peter ask the white cat how to get out of the garden? Though Peter doesn't listen to his mother, why does he pay attention to what his cousin has told him?
6. How does Peter finally get out of the garden? Can you think of other ways he might have escaped?
7. Do you think it was right for Mr. McGregor to try to catch Peter? Why or why not?
8. What causes Peter to be sick? What happens sometimes when we do things we are told not to do? Have you ever disobeyed your parents and been sorry?
*9. Do you think Peter will ever go into Mr. McGregor's garden again? Why or why not?

Art and Media

1. Have the children make a diorama window box to represent Mr. McGregor's garden. This can be done by planting vegetable seeds in a window box. On poster board have the children draw or paint the background of Mr. McGregor's garden: the fence, the tool shed, the scarecrow, etc. Place this in the back of the window box.
2. Collect various materials (velvet, cotton balls, construction paper, pieces of cloth, buttons, etc.) for Peter's clothes. Let

each child make a picture of Peter Rabbit using these materials. Allow the children to handle and discuss each other's pictures.

Creative Dramatics

1. Have the children pantomime the following movements of Peter Rabbit: (a) running fast on four legs to get away; (b) struggling to free himself from the gooseberry net; (c) wandering about lippity-lippity, looking all around; and (d) scuttering underneath the bushes.
2. Have children act out what might have happened if (a) Peter Rabbit had returned home with a bag of vegetables; (b) Peter Rabbit had talked to the cat; or (c) Flopsy, Mopsy, and Cottontail had gone with Peter.

Composing

1. Have the children make up stories about some of the other troubles Peter Rabbit might have encountered. Tape record these stories or write them on chart paper.
2. Below is a list of fruits and vegetables found in *The Tale of Peter Rabbit*. Have the children classify each as a fruit or a vegetable and arrange them in two columns on the board: currants, lettuce, blackberries, French beans, radishes, parsley, cucumbers, cabbage, potatoes, gooseberries, peas, onions.

Instructional Resources

Record—*The Tale of Peter Rabbit*, Scholastic (#4358), 33 rpm, $2.65. Includes copy of book.

Record—*The Tale of Peter Rabbit*, Caedmon (TC 1314), 33 rpm, $6.50. Includes four other Beatrix Potter stories.

Record—*The Tale of Peter Rabbit*, Weston Woods (LTR 33), 33 rpm, $1.95.

Record—*Peter Rabbit and the Tales of Beatrix Potter*, Angel (S-36789), 33 rpm, $6.98. John Lanchbery's original score for the Royal Ballet film, *Tales of Beatrix Potter*.

Cassette—*The Tale of Peter Rabbit*, Caedmon (CDL 51314), $7.95. Includes four other Beatrix Potter stories.

Cassette—*The Tale of Peter Rabbit*, Weston Woods (LTR 33C), $5.50.

Filmstrip—*The Tale of Peter Rabbit*, Weston Woods, $7.25 for filmstrip only (FS 33), $9.20 with record (SF 33), $12.75 with cassette (SF 33C).

Teaching Guide—"The Tale of Peter Rabbit," *A Curriculum for English, Grade 1* (Lincoln: University of Nebraska Press, 1966).

Sylvester and the Magic Pebble

By William Steig. (New York: Simon & Schuster, 1969. Available in paperback from E. P. Dutton & Co., Windmill Books.)

Summary

Sylvester, a donkey boy, finds a magic red pebble that grants all wishes. Frightened by a lion on his way home, he wishes that he were a rock. His wish is granted immediately. Sylvester remains a mute rock for a year until his parents luckily find him during a picnic on the rock. All are happily reunited. Themes: family love, security, acceptance of self.

Appraisal

Winner of the 1970 Caldecott Medal, this bright and colorful book is visually appealing to primary grade children. They also like its element of fantasy, its clever plot solution, and its focus on a small "person" who is rescued from insecurity by devoted parents. In most cases, the book should be read aloud.

Reading Considerations

Sylvester and the Magic Pebble is like many picture books—too difficult to be read independently by many first and second graders, but easily followed if read aloud by a teacher. Important words that may be unfamiliar include *usual* and *unusual, remarkable, ceased, disappear,* and *inquiring.*

Initiating Activities

1. Show children a brightly colored rock. Ask each of them what they might wish for if it were a magic rock.

2. Have two or more children act out a situation in which a worried mother and father are waiting up late for their little boy or girl, who was supposed to be home hours ago. Several groups of children might act out this problem and discuss the results.

Discussion Questions

1. When Sylvester becomes a rock, why isn't he able to change himself back into a donkey?
2. What do Sylvester's parents do when he doesn't come home? What would you have done in their place? What do you think your parents would have done?
*3. Why does Sylvester's mother say, "I will never scold Sylvester again as long as I live"? Would this have been a good idea?
4. How long does Sylvester remain a rock? How do you know? Of the three seasonal pictures (fall, winter, spring) of Sylvester as a rock, in which one do you think Sylvester is most lonely? Why?
5. Why do Mr. and Mrs. Duncan decide to go on a picnic? What are some of the things you do to make yourself feel better when you are sad?
6. How is Sylvester changed back into a donkey? Have you ever been separated from your parents for several days or longer? How did you feel when you saw them again?
7. Do you like the way the illustrator painted the sun on the next-to-last page? Why or why not?
*8. When they return home, why does Mr. Duncan put the magic pebble in an iron safe?
*9. Do Mr. and Mrs. Duncan love Sylvester very much? How do you know?

Art and Media

1. Have children make a pebble mosaic of Sylvester or of some scene in the book.
2. Let some children design a mural (with watercolors, poster paint, or actual materials—leaves, grass, etc.) depicting the passage of the seasons as Sylvester waits.

Creative Dramatics

1. After the children have heard the story two or three times, let them act out the last scene, beginning with the parents' decision to go on a picnic.
2. Have children improvise what might have happened if (a) Sylvester had not met the lion, but had taken the pebble home to his parents; or (b) at the picnic, Mr. Duncan had said, "I wish Sylvester were at home again," while holding the pebble.

Composing

1. Let children tape record what their thoughts and feelings might be if they were a large rock—from summer through fall, winter, and spring.
2. Have a group of children develop and record an ending based on what might have happened if Mr. and Mrs. Duncan had taken the magic pebble they found home with them. They might make a transcript of the new ending.
3. Have children collect a large number of pebbles and classify them according to shape, size, color, texture, etc. They might then select the group that looks most likely to be "magical," giving reasons for their choice.
4. On their picnic, Mr. and Mrs. Duncan take along a delicious donkey meal of alfalfa sandwiches, pickled oats, sassafras salad, and timothy compote. Have children write up a similar picnic menu for mice or rabbits.

Instructional Resources

Puppet Kit—*Sylvester and the Magic Pebble*, Society for Visual Education, $35.00. Includes two puppets, cassette, hardback book, and poster.

Mike Mulligan and His Steam Shovel

By Virginia Lee Burton. (Boston: Houghton Mifflin Co., 1939, 42 pp. Available in paperback from Houghton Mifflin Co.)

Summary

After years of accomplishment, Mike Mulligan and his beloved steam shovel Mary Anne are forced out of work by more modern machines. Given an opportunity, however, to dig the cellar for a new town hall in one day, they succeed—only to face one final problem, the solution of which provides both of them with a lifetime job. Themes: perseverance, ingenuity.

Appraisal

With its bright illustrations, clever ending, and personable characters (not the least of whom is Mary Anne herself), *Mike Mulligan and His Steam Shovel* has been a big favorite among children for over thirty-five years. It is one of the best examples of a children's story featuring an animated machine.

Reading Considerations

This is one of the less difficult picture books for primary grade children, many of whom should be able to read it by the end of the second grade. New words may include *canals, skyscraper, electric, Diesel, cellar, town hall, constable, furnace,* and *janitor.*

Initiating Activities

1. Visit an excavation site if possible. Direct the children's attention to power shovels in action. Or show the class a film or filmstrip about heavy machinery or construction.

17

2. Have one or more children bring a toy power shovel to class. Then let the class make up a story about one or several of the machines.

Discussion Questions

1. Do you think Mary Anne is a good name for a steam shovel? If you owned a steam shovel, what would you name it?
2. Why doesn't Mary Anne get old? Is it always true that if you take care of something it will not get old? Have you ever taken such good care of a toy that it lasted a long time?
3. When do Mike Mulligan and Mary Anne dig better and faster? Do you work better and faster when someone is watching you? Why or why not?
4. What kinds of machines take away Mary Anne's jobs? What other machines are no longer used because newer and bigger ones have taken their place?
*5. Why can't Mike Mulligan sell or throw away Mary Anne? Do you think he is silly to feel this way? Why or why not?
*6. Why does Henry B. Swap let Mike Mulligan and Mary Anne dig the basement of the town hall? Do you think he acted fairly? If you could meet Mr. Swap, what would you say to him?
7. How does the little boy's idea help Mary Anne and Mike finish their job on time? How does his second idea help Mike Mulligan get his money? Do children often or ever have better ideas than adults? Can you think of a time when this has happened?
8. Look at the second page from the end. How has the illustrator shown that everything is working out well?
*9. How does Henry B. Swap change? Why do you think that he and Mike Mulligan become friends?

Art and Media

1. Have children paint "sun faces" that match the scenes where Mike and Mary Anne are "VERY SAD" and where the little boy asks, "How are they going to get out?"
2. Let children design a poster advertising Mary Anne and her talents.
3. Several students might make shadow puppets of Mary Anne with moving parts (boom, dipper stick, etc.—note the separate

illustrations of these parts in the book). The puppets could then be used in drama activities.

Creative Dramatics

1. Let a child (or perhaps a group of children) pantomime a steam shovel in operation.
2. Using shadow puppets, let children act out the scene in which Mary Anne digs the basement for the town hall.
3. Have different students pretend to be Mike Mulligan and tell the class what he might have said to Mary Anne at the following places in the book: (a) when there are no more jobs, (b) when they get the job of digging the basement, (c) when they finish the job of digging the basement, or (d) as Mary Anne warms the town hall.

Composing

1. Have older children write a want ad for a steam shovel that could have appeared in the Popperville newspaper.
2. Consider letting children devise their own endings to the story. This teaching technique works especially well with *Mike Mulligan* because of the unique problem posed near its conclusion.
3. Mike Mulligan boasts that Mary Anne can do the work of one hundred men in one day. Have children make up some boasting statements about themselves and the members of their family and then have them tell whether or not they think those boasts could actually be proved.

Instructional Resources

Record—*Mike Mulligan and His Steam Shovel*, Weston Woods (LTR 4), 33 rpm, $1.95.
Cassette—*Mike Mulligan and His Steam Shovel*, Weston Woods (LTR 4C), $5.50.
Filmstrip—*Mike Mulligan and His Steam Shovel*, Weston Woods, $7.25 for filmstrip only (FS 4), $9.20 with record (SF 4), $12.75 with cassette (SF 4C).
Film—*Mike Mulligan and His Steam Shovel*, Weston Woods, 11 minutes, iconographic, color; $120.00 (sale), $5.00 (rental).

Why Mosquitoes Buzz in People's Ears

By Verna Aardema. Illustrated by Leo Dillon and Diane Dillon. (New York: Dial Press, 1975. Available in paperback from Scholastic Book Services.)

Summary

When Mosquito tells him a foolish story, Iguana puts sticks in his ears to keep from hearing. This sets in motion a series of hasty conclusions by several animals leading to the death of an owlet, the refusal of Mother Owl to wake the sun, and finally a trial, which retraces the series of mishaps back to the original source—the mosquito. Theme: the importance of communication.

Appraisal

Why Mosquitoes Buzz in People's Ears is a West African cumulative tale similar in design to "The Old Woman and Her Pig." It has a distinct flavor and appeal, to which plot and humor contribute significantly. Because of the Dillons' unique illustrations emphasizing movement and texture, the book won the Caldecott Medal for 1976.

Reading Considerations

Although this story has a lengthy plot and several characters, its refrain simplifies the narrative, making it quite accessible to first and second graders. Their response will be greater if the book is read aloud. Several of the animals may be unfamiliar (iguana, python, antelope), but each is well illustrated. Other important words include *council, alarmed,* and *guilty conscience.*

Initiating Activities

1. Have the children play the game of Gossip. Whisper a phrase or sentence in one child's ear and have him or her pass it on to the next child and so on around the circle. Have the last child in the group repeat the message aloud and compare it with the original message to see how it has changed. Emphasize the importance of giving and receiving messages carefully and completely.

2. Tell the class a pourquoi story about, for example, how the elephant got his trunk. Then ask questions like "How do you think the leopard got his spots?" and "Why do dogs turn around before lying down?" Finally, have the children talk about why mosquitoes buzz in people's ears.

Discussion Questions

1. Why does the iguana think that the mosquito's remark is nonsense? What else might he have done besides putting sticks in his ears?

*2. Of the four animals that flee (python, rabbit, crow, monkey), which do you think has the best reason? The worst? Why?

3. Look at the picture of the tree limb breaking. How does the limb look different from the one on the opposite page?

*4. How does Mother Owl feel about what happens when the limb breaks? Was it right for her to refuse to wake the sun? Why or why not? What else might she have done?

5. Why does King Lion call the council meeting?

6. How does Mother Owl find out who killed her owlet? How does she think it happened? How does what she thinks differ from what really happened? (Look at the picture where Mother Owl "thinks about" the incident.)

*7. Why does each animal blame another one? Is it all right to blame other people for something that goes wrong? Why or why not? Have you ever been wrongly blamed for something you didn't do? How did you feel?

8. Look at the picture of the rabbit under the dark trees. How have the illustrators made him look as though he's running very fast?

9. Why hadn't the iguana come to the meeting?

*10. Do you think the monkey is any more to blame than the other animals? Why or why not? Who *is* to blame? Why do you think Mother Owl is finally satisfied? Why is the sun winking when it comes back up?

11. Why does the mosquito ask to this day if people are still angry? Do you answer her the same way?

Art and Media

1. The sun often observes the incidents in this book. Have the children draw a picture of the sun as it might have looked on the last page of the book if it had seen what happens to the mosquito.

2. Direct children in the drawing of "movement pictures," like the one of the limb breaking and falling. Suggest possibilities: a tree falling, a flower growing, a balloon expanding and bursting, etc.

Creative Dramatics

1. Let several children pantomime the story as it is read aloud. When the council meeting begins, they can add dialogue.

2. Have children act out what would have happened if the mosquito had been brought to the council meeting. Roles might include Mosquito, King Lion, Mother Owl, Iguana, and Monkey.

Composing

1. Let children write or dictate a story for one of the following:
   a. Why the Python Goes Wasawusu, Wasawusu,
   b. Why the Rabbit Has Long Ears,
   c. Why Owls Hoot at Night.

2. Encourage able readers in the class to find out why (or how) mosquitoes really do buzz in people's ears. They might use a children's encyclopedia, writing down brief notes to report to the class. (Younger children might ask their parents and contribute to a dictated class report the following day.)

3. Most of the animals at the council meeting remain silent. Let children write what some of the animals might be thinking. The scene where the crow explains himself would be especially

appropriate, particularly for the antelope, the monkey, and the giraffe.

Instructional Resources

Record—*Why Mosquitoes Buzz in People's Ears*, Miller-Brody Productions (7-WM 100), 33 rpm, $6.95.

Cassette—*Why Mosquitoes Buzz in People's Ears*, Miller-Brody Productions (7-WM 100C), $7.95.

Cassette—*Why Mosquitoes Buzz in People's Ears*, Weston Woods (LTR 199C), $5.50.

Filmstrip—*Why Mosquitoes Buzz in People's Ears,* Weston Woods, $7.25 for filmstrip only (FS 199), $12.75 with cassette (SF 199C).

Record-Book Combination—*Why Mosquitoes Buzz in People's Ears*, Scholastic Book Services (20789), 33 rpm, $2.65.

Puppet Kit—*Why Mosquitoes Buzz in People's Ears*, Society for Visual Education, $35.00; includes two puppets, cassette, hardback book, and poster.

The Biggest Bear

By Lynd Ward. (Boston: Houghton Mifflin Co., 1952, 84 pp. Available in paperback from Houghton Mifflin Co.)

Summary

Johnny Orchard is humiliated because his family does not have a bearskin on their barn. One day he finds a bear cub which becomes his pet. However, the bear soon grows too large and too destructive, and because he refuses to return to the woods, Johnny is faced with the responsibility of shooting him. Fortunately, the bear is captured and taken to a zoo where Johnny can visit him frequently. Themes: responsibility, love of animals.

Appraisal

A Caldecott winner in 1953, *The Biggest Bear* has achieved widespread popularity among children from four to ten and critical acclaim for its dramatic full-page illustrations in brown and white and its adventurous story of a small boy faced with a large responsibility. The book is lively, humorous, and suspenseful.

Reading Considerations

The Biggest Bear can be read independently by many children in the primary grades. Although certain regional terms (*maple sugar, smokehouse, sap bucket, tapping*) may be unfamiliar, only the word *humiliated* might be discussed before reading.

Initiating Activities

1. Ask the children to imagine that they have a favorite cat. This cat is always getting into trouble by scratching the furniture

and knocking things over. Explain to the children that now their mother or father says they must give the cat away. Ask the children how they would feel and what they would say or do. Have them act out the scene between parent and child.

2. Ask the children to imagine they are going to a big party with all their relatives. Their mothers dress them in silly, frilly clothes while the other children are dressed in comfortable clothes, like jeans and T-shirts. In addition, their mothers treat them like babies and will not let them have fun with the other children. Ask how they would feel. Discuss the meaning of humiliation. Allow children to share other humiliating experiences if they wish.

Discussion Questions

1. Why does Johnny want a bearskin? What things have you ever wanted because everyone else had one?
*2. Was Johnny's grandfather wise to run from the bear? How does Johnny feel about what his grandfather did? What should you do if you meet a bear in the woods?
3. Why isn't the young bear a good pet? What animals make good pets? What animals do not make good pets?
4. Why does the bear continue to return to Johnny's home? How does the bear get back from the island without getting wet?
*5. Why does it take Johnny so long to get the bullet in his gun? What kinds of things do you do to put off unpleasant jobs?
6. How is the bear captured? In what other ways do men capture animals?
*7. Do you think Johnny feels good about what happens to his bear at the end of the book? Do you think he feels good about himself? Why or why not?

Art and Media

1. Have children draw several different sketches of the biggest bear to illustrate how he grew. They may use pencils, crayons, or felt-tip markers. These drawings might be done on newsprint or butcher paper.
2. Provide large brown paper bags or materials for making papier-mâché masks for the children so that they may make bear masks. (These may be used in the creative dramatics activities.)

Creative Dramatics

1. Ask each child to pretend to be the biggest bear. Have them move around the classroom as the bear might have. Then ask various children to pretend to be the biggest bear in the following places: (a) Johnny's mother's kitchen, (b) the smokehouse with bacon and hams, and (c) the shed with bottles of maple syrup.
2. Choose several children to play Mr. McLean, Mr. Pennell, Mr. Carroll, Johnny, and his father. Ask them to enact the scene in which the men complain about the bear to Johnny and his father. If needed, provide time before they start for discussion of what each person might say.
3. Ask children to pretend to be the biggest bear telling the story of how he met Johnny and came to live at his house.

Composing

1. Have children make a list of different kinds of bears. Then have them research the types of bears and prepare a chart telling what each kind eats, where it lives, how large it grows, and so on.
2. Take the children on a field trip to a local zoo to observe the bears. When they return to the classroom, let the group write an experience story about their observations.
3. Discuss how maple syrup is made. If possible, let each child taste some maple sugar. Ask the children to write or tell step-by-step instructions for making maple sugar.

Instructional Resources

Record—*The Biggest Bear*, Weston Woods (LTR 10), 33 rpm, $1.95.
Cassette—*The Biggest Bear*, Weston Woods, (LTR 10C), $5.50.
Filmstrip—*The Biggest Bear*, Weston Woods, $7.25 for filmstrip only (FS 10), $9.20 with record (SF 10), $12.75 with cassette (SF 10C).

Crow Boy

By Taro Yashima. (New York: Viking Press, 1955, 37 pp. Available in paperback from Viking Press.)

Summary

A small, shy Japanese boy named Chibi spends his first five years of school isolated and taunted by his classmates, who do not understand him. Encouraged by a sympathetic teacher in the sixth grade, Chibi reveals his uniqueness and sensitivity at a talent show through his ingenious imitations of crows, and thereby gains the acceptance of his classmates. Themes: rejection and acceptance.

Appraisal

Crow Boy is a sensitive, compassionate picture book dealing with a theme of relevance to all children. It is one of the few picture books with genuine character development.

Reading Considerations

Some second grade and many third grade children could read *Crow Boy* independently. Challenging words include *forlorn, interesting, trudging, admired, announced, imagine, graduation, attendance,* and *charcoal.* But the most important word by far is *imitate.*

Initiating Activity

Have a group of children form a circle with arms linked. Select an individual child to try for a few seconds to break into the circle. After the "rejected" child tells how it felt to be momentarily left out, the class can discuss feelings of acceptance and rejection.

Discussion Questions

1. At the beginning, why is Chibi hiding under the school? Have you ever wanted to hide somewhere at school? Why?
2. Why do you think Chibi is afraid?
3. How do the other children feel about him?
4. Why did the artist make the picture on page 11 seem shaky? Why does Chibi cross his eyes? What does he not want to see?
5. Do you think Chibi is a good student? Do you think he is stupid? How does he seem to learn about things?
*6. Why do you think Chibi comes to school every day even though he feels alone? Would you have done this?
*7. Why does Mr. Isobe like and admire Chibi?
8. What different kinds of crows does Chibi imitate at the talent show? Why do you think he does so many? How does his performance affect the people who listen? Why do they cry?
*9. Is the boy at the end of the book different from the boy at the beginning? In what ways?
10. Have you ever known any children who seemed lonely and sad at school? How were they treated by others? How can children like these be helped?

Art and Media

1. After consulting a reference book on origami (the Japanese art of folding paper), have children make paper crows that might be used to construct a mobile.
2. Let the class cut out pictures of children from magazines and design montages that express the idea of being alone.

Creative Dramatics

1. Let three children act out a situation in which they are Crow Boy as a first or second grader and his parents. One day when he comes home from school, they ask him what he did in school that day.
2. Ask children to pantomime how Chibi walked ("trudged") to school early in the book and then how he "set off for his home on the far side of the mountain" at the end. Emphasize the difference.
3. Have the children improvise one of the conversations between Chibi and Mr. Isobe.

Composing

1. Have children look at the ceiling, their desk top, someone's shirt, or out the window and make a list of things they "see." Post these on the bulletin board, as Mr. Isobe did with Chibi's list.
2. Crow Boy's specialty is imitating crows. Ask each child to think of something special that he or she knows about and to tell about it or demonstrate it for the group.
3. The nickname Crow Boy is given to Chibi when his talent for imitating crows is discovered. Let students compose stories imagining how the following nicknames might have originated: Flipper, Slugger, Wonder Woman, Tarzan.

Instructional Resources

Record—*Crow Boy*, Weston Woods (LTR 42), 33 rpm, $1.95.

Cassette—*Crow Boy*, Weston Woods (LTR 42C), $5.50.

Cassette (with books)—*Crow Boy*, Miller-Brody Productions (7-VRB 24933-7), $17.95. Includes eight paperback copies of book.

Filmstrip—*Crow Boy*, Weston Woods, $7.25 for filmstrip only (FS 42), $9.20 with record (SF 42), $12.75 with cassette (SF 42C).

Film—*Crow Boy,* Weston Woods, 13 minutes, iconographic, color; $135.00 (sale), $6.00 (rental).

Teaching Guide—Charlotte S. Huck, *Children's Literature in the Elementary School*, 3rd ed. (New York: Holt, Rinehart and Winston, 1976), pp. 722-23.

Teaching Guide—"Crow Boy," *A Curriculum for English, Grade 2* (Lincoln: University of Nebraska Press, 1966).

One Morning in Maine

By Robert McCloskey. (New York: Viking Press, 1952, 64 pp. Available in paperback from Viking Press.)

Summary

Sal wakes up one morning anticipating a boat trip to Buck's Harbor with her father. The events that result from her discovery and subsequent loss of a loose tooth help her to realize that she is growing up and becoming capable of increased responsibilities. Themes: growing up, family life.

Appraisal

Set beautifully along the coast of Maine, this book is a warm and comfortable favorite of many children from four to eight. The text and illustrations are realistic, the latter being pen-and-ink sketches of dark blue and white. *One Morning in Maine* was a runner-up for the Caldecott Medal in 1953.

Reading Considerations

Like many picture books, *One Morning in Maine* is too difficult for most primary grade children to read independently. Some important words that might be introduced to children include *clams, sympathized, reluctantly, definitely, clam chowder, outboard motor, dictated, harbor,* and *appetite.*

Initiating Activities

1. In small groups, give each child the opportunity to respond to the question, "What happens when a tooth comes out?"

2. If possible, show children what clams are. It would be instructive if they could taste clam chowder—ideally by making some themselves in class.

Discussion Questions

1. How does Sal feel when she wakes up? What makes her feel this way? Would you feel (or have you felt) this way when you lost a tooth?
*2. Look at the picture on pages 14-15. What has Jane done? How does she feel about it? How does her mother feel about it? What do you think Jane's mother will do?
3. Why does Sal tell several birds and animals about her loose tooth on the way to the beach?
4. How does Sal help her father? How does she feel about helping her father? In what ways do you help your parents? How will you help them as you get bigger?
5. How do Sal's parents help her when she discovers her loose tooth? What else might they have said or done?
6. Sal's father tells her that big girls don't cry about losing a tooth. What things do little boys and girls cry about? What things do big boys and girls cry about?
*7. How is the sea gull like Sal? How does the sea gull help Sal without even knowing it? Why are the animals—the loons, the seal, and the clams—important to Sal and her family?
8. How does Sal help her little sister? How do you help your younger brothers and sisters or other children that you know? Does someone have to tell you to be helpful or do you do these things by yourself?
9. As you grow up, parts of your body change. What changes have you noticed? What other changes do you expect?
*10. Do you think Sal has "grown up" any in just one day? Why or why not?

Art and Media

1. Let a group of children paint a mural (using tempera and shelf paper) of the coastline from Sal's house to the point where her father is digging for clams (pp. 16-29).

2. Encourage some children to make a collage based on the idea of families or growing up.

Creative Dramatics

1. Have children pantomime the scene in which Sal, Jane, and their father take the boat trip to Buck's Harbor.
2. In the book Sal is worried about her loose tooth, and her mother explains to her why this is happening. Have children improvise scenes of similar anxiety in which parents must explain things to children, such as why a friend has to move away or why we have to get vaccinated.

Composing

1. Let children dictate stories to the teacher: (a) about personal experiences with lost teeth, (b) about what might have happened if, for example, Sal had not lost her tooth, (c) about younger brother or sisters, (d) about "One Morning in _____."
2. Have children look at the picture on pages 52-53 and list as many things as they can under the heading "tools"; or, using pages 14-15, list things under the headings "furniture" or "kitchen items."
3. Sal wishes for a chocolate ice cream cone. Have students write a note to a friend explaining how they, like Sal, lost a tooth, and telling what they wished for, whether they got exactly what they wished for, or whether they got something that was not quite so good, or something even better.

Arrow to the Sun
A Pueblo Indian Tale

By Gerald McDermott. (New York: Viking Press, 1974. Available in paperback from Penguin Books.)

Summary

Mocked by his playmates for having no father, a Pueblo Indian boy sets out to find him. He is helped in his search by Arrow Maker, who launches him as an arrow to the sun. There the Boy finds his father, endures four trials required of him, and returns to earth filled with the power of the sun. Themes: the importance of overcoming obstacles, courage.

Appraisal

Arrow to the Sun won the Caldecott Award for 1975. Its bold patterns and colors, dominated by the earth tones of yellow, orange, and brown, dramatically reinforce a Pueblo Indian initiation tale that should appeal to children in grades one through three, many of whom will perceive the story as an example of the child overcoming adversity.

Reading Considerations

Although this book is accessible to many second and third graders in terms of its vocabulary and uncomplicated sentence structure, the plot is more difficult than that of most picture books. Some of the incidents (like the Lord of the Sun shooting the spark of life to earth) may require explanation. Important words that might be discussed before reading include *pueblo, mocked, kiva,* and *transformed.*

Initiating Activities

1. Show children the two-page illustration where the Boy is shot into the heavens toward the sun. Ask them what they think the book might be about.
2. Have the children talk about which one of the following would frighten them the most (or least): a roomful of bees, of snakes, of lions, or of lightning.

Discussion Questions

1. How does the Boy come into the world of men? Why do you think the Lord of the Sun wanted to send the spark of life to earth?
2. The Boy is mocked because he has no father. How does the illustrator of the book make the Boy and his mother look sad? What does the Boy do when he is teased? Was this the best thing to do? What else could he have done? What might you have done?
3. Why do you think Corn Planter and Pot Maker refuse to help the Boy? Why does Arrow Maker agree to help?
4. How does the Boy change in becoming the arrow? (Look at the picture.)
*5. Do you think the Boy is brave? Why or why not?
6. As the Boy travels to the sun, he passes by many stars. Why do you think the stars become more colorful as he gets nearer the sun?
*7. Why is the Lord of the Sun so colorful? Why does he require the Boy to pass the four tests?
8. Which one of the four trials do you think is the hardest? Why? Can you think of others that would be harder? Why do you think the lightning trial is the last one?
9. Why does the Lord of the Sun shoot the Boy to earth again?
*10. How has the Boy changed during the story? Why do the people celebrate his return?
*11. Do you think the Lord of the Sun will punish Corn Planter and Pot Maker? Should he? Why or why not?

Art and Media

1. Give the children a sheet of paper on which are drawn two outlines of the Boy's face. Let them draw the Boy's expression

(a) when he is teased by his playmates and (b) later when he returns from the sun.
2. Let the children make collages of other kinds of animals and forces that might have served as dangerous and difficult trials for the Boy.
3. Let children draw their own Pueblo Indian designs like those on the inside cover of the book. (Also see Composing #2.)

Creative Dramatics

1. Lead children in performing the Dance of Life with which the Indians celebrate the Boy's return. Appropriate Indian music might be used.
2. Have several children act out a scene where the Boy meets his playmates again after his return from the sun. What would he tell them about his adventure? How would they react?
3. Let groups of children pantomime the Boy's four trials against the lions, the serpents, the bees, and the lightning.

Composing

1. Let children write or dictate instructions that Arrow Maker might give for creating an arrow from a boy. Give them a beginning: "First the boy must stand up straight and tall."
2. Have children examine the Boy's special sign. Ask them what it might be. Then let them draw and write about a similar sign that they would like for themselves.

Instructional Resources

Cassette—*Arrow to the Sun*, Weston Woods (LTR 184C), $5.50.
Filmstrip—*Arrow to the Sun*, Weston Woods, $7.25 for filmstrip only (FS 184), $12.75 with cassette (SF184C).

Sam, Bangs, and Moonshine

By Evaline Ness. (New York: Holt, Rinehart and Winston, 1966. Available in paperback from Holt, Rinehart and Winston.)

Summary

Samantha's reckless habit of lying gets her into trouble when gullible Thomas believes her "MOONSHINE" and heads for the cave behind Blue Rock to find Sam's imaginary baby kangaroo. A storm comes up and both Thomas and Sam's cat, Bangs, barely escape. Sam's concern for them leads her to make distinctions between good "MOONSHINE" and bad "MOONSHINE." Themes: fantasy and reality.

Appraisal

This Caldecott winner accurately portrays the world of children, which blends the fantastic and the real. Children in the primary grades enjoy both the story and the engaging illustrations done in shades of black, green, and gold.

Reading Considerations

For the most part, this book should be read to children. More capable readers who attempt it on their own may have trouble with these words: *scoured, massive, chariot, menacing, torrents,* and *sodden.*

Initiating Activities

1. Ask the children if they know any people who like to tell lies. Let them discuss some of the lies these people tell. Ask if these lies ever have hurt anyone or could hurt anyone. Discuss the possible dangers in telling lies.

2. Ask the children to think about their secret worlds where they can do or be anything they want. You may want to discuss some common fantasies as a starting point. Then ask the children to draw pictures of their secret worlds, using pencils or felt-tip pens. Allow any child who wishes to share and discuss his or her drawing with the group.

Discussion Questions

*1. Sam makes up stories about the things around her. Why does she do this? Does she have many exciting things in her life?
 2. Sam's father tells her to stop talking "MOONSHINE." What does he mean? Why doesn't Sam understand what he means?
*3. What does Thomas have that Sam doesn't have? Why does Thomas believe all the things that Sam says? Why does he always go wherever Sam tells him to go?
 4. Does Sam know it is dangerous for Thomas to go to Blue Rock to look for the baby kangaroo? Would she have sent him if she had known? Why does Bangs go after Thomas?
 5. How does Sam's father feel when she tells him about Thomas and Bangs? What does he do?
 6. Why does it seem like such a long time before Sam's father comes back? Have you ever waited for something to happen? Did it seem to take a long time even though it may have been a short time?
*7. How does Sam learn the difference between reality and "MOONSHINE"? Do you think this is a hard lesson for her to learn? Why or why not?
 8. How does Bangs escape from the storm and get home? Have you ever heard the expression "A cat has nine lives"? What does it mean?
 9. Why does Sam think the gerbil is a kangaroo? Look at the pictures of him. In what ways does he look like a kangaroo? What does Sam do with the gerbil? Why does she do this?
*10. Is all "MOONSHINE" bad? What is good "MOONSHINE"?

Art and Media

1. Ask the children to draw or paint what they think a lie would look like if they could see one when it is told. Have them use fingerpaint, crayons, or tempera. Ask them what color a lie is, what shape it has, how much of their paper it would take

up, and so on. (If this seems too abstract, ask the children to think of a lie as a form coming from a person's mouth, like the balloons in comic strips.)

2. Let the children use watercolors to draw a picture of a familiar scene in a heavy rain. Ask them to explain the difference between the scene in the rain and on a sunny day.

Creative Dramatics

1. Ask several pairs of children to act out the scene between Sam and Thomas when she makes up stories about where the baby kangaroo is. Have them think about the way Sam would talk and the way Thomas would answer her.

2. Play "The Biggest Lie Game." Have one child start a story which contains an exaggeration or a lie. The next child is to stretch the truth further and the next even further. When the group agrees that the truth can be stretched no further, the next child may start a new story. Example: *Child 1*: My mother is very big. She is as big as a bear. She picks up trees with her bare hands. *Child 2*: My mother is as big as a barn. She can move a whole house by herself. *Child 3*: My mother is as big as a mountain. She can carry a whole town full of people on her back, etc.

Composing

1. Sam made up stories about the things around her: her mother, the cat, the rug on the doorstep. Ask the children to pick out several objects in the classroom, list these objects, and write an experience story about what these things might be or do.

2. Sam had to learn the difference between reality and "MOONSHINE." Below is a list of objects. Ask the children to classify these as "real" or "MOONSHINE":
   a. a car that flies,
   b. a family on a camping trip,
   c. a princess who slept for one hundred years,
   d. a lost dog,
   e. a donkey that turns into a stone,
   f. a rabbit that can talk.
   You may extend this activity by asking the children to change the objects, making the real ones "MOONSHINE" and vice versa. You may also have the class add more items to each list.

Instructional Resources

Cassette—*Sam, Bangs and Moonshine*, Miller-Brody Productions (7-FAC 110), $7.95.
Filmstrip—*Sam, Bangs and Moonshine*, Miller-Brody Productions, $16.00 with record (7-FA 110) or with cassette (7-FA 110C).

The Hundred Penny Box

By Sharon Bell Mathis. Illustrated by Leo Dillon and Diane Dillon. (New York: Viking Press, 1975, 47 pp.)

Summary

When Michael's great-great-aunt Dew moves into his parents' house, his mother Ruth has difficulty adjusting to the elderly lady, who insists on keeping her old things around her. Ruth especially wants to replace Aunt Dew's hundred penny box, which contains one penny from each year of Aunt Dew's life. Michael, who loves and understands his great-great-aunt, works out a way to preserve her treasure. Themes: youth and old age, family relationships.

Appraisal

This inspiring little book presents a vivid picture of the close relationship between an old woman and a young boy. Although *The Hundred Penny Box* is not a picture book, the stunning brown-toned watercolor illustrations by Leo and Diane Dillon enhance the story and contribute significantly toward making it an effective bridge between picture books and longer novels.

Reading Considerations

The simple vocabulary and syntax of *The Hundred Penny Box* make it an excellent book for third and fourth grade students to read independently. The few words that may be unfamiliar include *Victrola* (p. 16), *britches* (23), *irritable* (33), *mahogany* (33), and *frail* (40).

Initiating Activities

1. After reading a book like *Annie and the Old One* by Miska Miles to the children, let them draw pictures of an elderly person they know doing something with them that they both enjoy. Have them save their pictures to compare with the illustrations in *The Hundred Penny Box*.
2. Discuss with the children the following questions: Have you ever had an object that you loved get broken, lost, or thrown away? How did you feel when this happened? Did you find something else to take its place?

Discussion Questions

*1. Why has Aunt Dew come to live with Michael and his parents? How do the parents' feelings toward her differ? Is it right for Ruth to feel as she does? Why or why not?
2. Why do you think Aunt Dew sings her favorite song so often?
3. Why does Ruth want to throw away Aunt Dew's hundred penny box? Why does Michael want to save it?
*4. Aunt Dew says, "Anybody takes my hundred penny box takes me!" What does she mean by this?
5. Years before, what had happened to John's parents? Why had John taken the boat apart?
*6. What do Michael and Aunt Dew enjoy doing with the pennies? Why does Michael enjoy doing it? Why does Aunt Dew? Why is she so attached to the box and its contents?
7. Look at the illustration on page 27. Who are the people pictured there? Why is the top part of the picture darker and harder to see?
*8. Why does Ruth want Aunt Dew to take her nap? Why does Aunt Dew cry? How does Ruth explain her crying to Michael? Why does Michael become angry? Have you ever argued with your parents about how someone else in the family was treated?
*9. How is Aunt Dew's box like Michael's teddy bear? How is it different?
10. Is it wrong for Michael to want to hide the box? Why or why not?

11. What kinds of things does Aunt Dew forget? What things does she remember? Why does she forget some things and remember others? What kinds of things do you most easily forget or remember?
12. What do you think will happen to the hundred penny box? Why?

Art and Media

1. Have each child prepare a "self" box that represents his or her own life. Pictures, snapshots, or real objects could be glued or fastened to the box or placed inside. When finished, the boxes might be shared with the class.
2. The illustrations in this book are watercolors applied with cotton, with light areas created by water and bleach applied with a brush. Have children create additional illustrations with watercolor paints and cotton swabs (of Michael and his father, for example; or of the children's own family life).

Creative Dramatics

1. Pantomime with the children the movements that Aunt Dew makes to her record; use, perhaps, a recording of "Take My Hand, Precious Lord." Help the children imagine how her age would affect her ability to move.
2. Let children act out one of the following scenes between Michael and Aunt Dew: (a) the two of them counting the pennies, (b) Michael trying to get Aunt Dew to hide the hundred penny box, or (c) Michael asking her to tell stories.
3. Have three children improvise a scene in which Ruth brings to Aunt Dew her one hundred pennies—now placed in the tiny mahogany chest. Roles: Ruth, Aunt Dew, Michael.

Composing

1. Have children write a description of something they own that is old but still precious to them. It might be a toy, a book, or perhaps something they found. Have them describe the item exactly as it is—including any rips, holes, spots, or other defects—and tell why they value the object even though it may seem to be worthless to anyone else.

2. Encourage children to write a very short biography of one of their older relatives—a grandparent, or perhaps an aunt or uncle. Suggest that they list important events by the years in which they happened, as Aunt Dew did.
3. As Aunt Dew remembers her home, everything was the biggest and the best. Let children write statements about their school, their home, their best friend, and their parents as Aunt Dew would have remembered them.
4. Have children write a diamante poem about youth and old age or about children and grandparents. A diamante is a diamond-shaped pattern poem based on contrasts. The pattern produces a seven-line poem following these specifications: 1 word—subject noun; 2 words—adjectives; 3 words—participles (*-ing*, *-ed*); 4 words—nouns related to the subject; 3 words—participles; 2 words—adjectives; 1 word—noun (opposite of the subject). For example:

Earth

Lovely, awesome,

Spinning, changing, greening,

Land,   ocean,   air,   night,

Expanding, shooting, darkening,

Lonely, starry,

Space

Instructional Resources

Record—*The Hundred Penny Box*, Miller-Brody Productions (7-NAR 3106), 33 rpm, $6.95.

Cassette—*The Hundred Penny Box*, Miller-Brody Productions (7-NAC 3106), $7.95.

The Courage of Sarah Noble

By Alice Dalgliesh. Illustrated by Leonard Weisgard. (New York: Charles Scribner's Sons, 1954, 54 pp. Available in paperback from Charles Scribner's Sons.)

Summary

In 1707, eight-year-old Sarah Noble and her father set out from Massachusetts for their new home in New Milford, Connecticut. Bravely Sarah stays with her father, cooks for him, and even remains with friendly Indians when he goes back to Massachusetts to get the rest of the family. Themes: courage, conquering the wilderness, understanding other cultures.

Appraisal

This simple tale of a brave young girl facing the unknown dangers of the wilderness is heartwarming and charming. Children in the intermediate grades (3-4) can find in Sarah an admirable character who is kind and good and who overcomes the fears and anxieties common to us all.

Reading Considerations

The vocabulary and syntactic patterns of this book are such that most children in the intermediate grades could read the book independently. New vocabulary words might include *solemn* (pp. 14, 37), *outlandish* (50), and *porridge* (20).

Initiating Activities

1. Darken the room as much as possible and ask the children to imagine that they are in a forest at night. Play a tape or record

of typical night noises, such as crickets chirping, owls hooting, frogs croaking. (Possible recordings include *Wait 'til the Moon Is Full*, available from Learning Arts, and *Voices of the Night*, available from Cornell University.) Ask the children to be perfectly still as they listen to these noises. Then let them discuss how they felt.

2. Play a record of a story or conversation in a foreign language. Have the class discuss how they would feel if they went to a country where no one speaks English. Or, if possible, have someone who speaks a foreign language come in and talk to the class.

Discussion Questions

1. Why do Sarah and her father set out on their journey alone?
*2. Why do Sarah and her father look forward to sleeping at the Robinsons' house, even though the people are unfriendly? Why do you think Sarah chooses to keep her cloak on?
3. What stories do the Robinson children tell about the Indians? How does Sarah feel when she hears these stories? Were you ever frightened by stories even though you felt sure they weren't true?
*4. How does Sarah know there is no love in the Robinson house? What does her father mean when he says Sarah is too wise for her years?
5. What does Sarah's new home look like when she first arrives? How do you think she feels? Can you remember how you felt when you first saw a new place you had heard a lot about?
6. How does Sarah's father make the cave comfortable? What objects would you consider necessary to make a place comfortable?
*7. What does Sarah feel when the Indian children first come upon her? What causes her to feel this way? Do you think that Sarah is impolite to the Indian children? Why or why not?
8. How do Sarah and the Indian children help each other? In what ways might they have helped each other?
9. Why must Sarah stay behind when her father leaves? How does Sarah feel about staying with the Indians? How would you feel?
*10. How has Sarah changed by the time her family returns? Does she look different? Does she act different? In what ways is she the same?

*11. Sarah says she has become a woman. In what ways is this true?

12. Throughout the book Sarah's father wonders if he has done the right thing. Do you think he did? Why or why not?

*13. Sarah keeps saying to herself, "Keep up your courage, Sarah Noble." What objects, people, and things help her to keep up her courage?

Art and Media

1. Let the class make a quilt, such as the one Sarah Noble sleeps on during her journey. Each child should design individual patches that tell something about themselves. The children can then sew the patches together and display the quilt.

2. Have children construct dioramas—using cardboard, construction paper, twigs, and bark—of Sarah's new home and Indian John's home. They should furnish the dwellings realistically and discuss how each is suitable for the people who lived there.

Creative Dramatics

1. Have several students act out the scene in which Sarah meets the Indian children. They should try to show how Sarah's attitude toward them changes and how they react to her.

2. Let small groups make up a skit about one of the following:
   a. meeting someone new and strange,
   b. greeting someone you love very much whom you haven't seen for a long time,
   c. being teased about something you are afraid of or uncertain about.

Composing

1. Encourage children to write three entries in a diary that Sarah might have kept. They may choose three consecutive days or pick any three exciting days to write about.

2. Have the children write a letter that Sarah might have written and sent to her mother. Choose one of the following times when Sarah might have written:
   a. after her first night in the forest,
   b. after her stay at the Robinsons' house,

    c. after she first met the Indians,

    d. when her father was returning for the rest of the family.

3. Indian John was noted for not wasting words, even when he spoke in his own language. For example, in Chapter 10, instead of saying to Sarah, "Your parents are waiting for you now. You should hurry to your house to meet them. We feel that you are like a daughter to us," Indian John says, "You go, now, my daughter." Ask children to write the following passages from the book as concisely as Indian John might have said them.

    a. "It was a blessing the Lord gave me daughters, as well as sons. And one of them all of eight years old, and a born cook."

    b. "Mistress Robinson should teach her children to watch their words. She should watch her own. And there are people in this world who do not help others along the way, Sarah, while there are others who do."

    c. "And when I came back I found Sarah as clean and well-dressed as when I left her. Tall John's wife is almost as careful as you, Mary."

4. Let the children write or tell what happened to Sarah when she grew up. Did she move to a city? Did she have a job? Did she remember her Indian friends? Did she get married and have a family?

Instructional Resources

Teaching Guide—"The Courage of Sarah Noble," *A Curriculum for English, Grade 3* (Lincoln: University of Nebraska Press, 1966).

The Matchlock Gun

By Walter D. Edmonds. Illustrated by Paul Lantz. (New York: Dodd, Mead & Co., 1941, 50 pp.)

Summary

When Teunis Van Alstyne leaves his family to guard a bridge against Indian attack in the Hudson River valley, his wife Gertrude and the two children are left alone in their isolated house. On the following day, as the Indians seem to be drawing near, Gertrude prepares to defend their house. She shows ten-year-old Edward how to fire the huge matchlock gun that hangs so impressively over the fireplace. That evening Edward repels the Indian attack with the gun he has so long admired. Themes: responsibility, courage.

Appraisal

The Matchlock Gun won the Newbery Medal in 1942 largely because of its suspenseful plot, memorable style, and sensitive portrayal of a family determined to protect itself against one of the frontier's harsh realities. Although they are not always appropriately located in the text, Paul Lantz's color illustrations of firelit darkness effectively convey a mood of high drama. Despite its setting and faithfulness to history, *The Matchlock Gun* has been criticized by some who say it depicts Indians as bloodthirsty savages and emphasizes violence.

Reading Considerations

This book will not be easy for third and fourth graders, though some can read it independently. Many of the words will be unfamiliar. The book is short enough, however, to be easily read aloud by the teacher in two or three sittings. Some of the more important words include *militia* (pp. 1, 2, 6, 16, 49), *musket* (2, 4, 6, 19, 27), *mechanically* (11), *solitary* (16), *secure* (17), and *primed* or *priming* (4, 30, 34, 44).

Initiating Activities

1. Have each student put on a blindfold. Tell the students not to remove their blindfolds or move around until you say the word "children." Then walk to the door and pretend to leave the room. After a minute or so of silence, say words like "church," "chirp," "chill," and finally "children." Afterwards, have them talk about how hard it was for them to follow your instructions.
2. Have class members think of a time when they were afraid. Have them tell what caused them to be afraid, how they felt, and how, eventually, their fears were eased.

Discussion Questions

1. How old is Edward? How does he feel about the matchlock gun? Why does he want his father to take it? Why isn't it a good gun for his father to use?
2. Why does Gertrude refuse to go to the Widow Van Alstyne's house?
*3. In the loft, how do Gertrude and Edward feel about Father being away? Calm? Worried? Afraid? (Do they admit they're afraid?) Is Trudy worried? How would you have felt?
*4. Gertrude thinks that Trudy is "too young to notice things." What kinds of things does Edward notice that make him helpful?
5. Why does Gertrude remain outside during the day?
6. What are some of the things that cause Gertrude to grow more worried as the day passes? Why does she decide to remain at the house?
7. How does Gertrude prepare to defend the house?
*8. How does Edward feel about the instructions his mother gives? Is he afraid? Is he brave? Can a person be both afraid and brave at the same time? Does his mother have faith in Edward? Why is she so concerned?
9. Why is Gertrude so careful about how fast she runs toward the house?
*10. Besides firing the gun, what does Edward do that shows how brave and smart he is? Have you ever been asked by your

parents to do something very important? What was it? How did you feel about it? Did you succeed?

Art and Media

1. In his mind's eye, Edward sees the hams hanging from the roof above the loft as approaching French soldiers. Using black paper, help the children draw and cut out silhouettes of the Indians (see pp. 35, 40) and paste them against backgrounds of appropriate gift-wrapping paper to help convey the feeling of fear and excitement felt by the Van Alstynes.
2. Let the children who wish make a handkerchief doll like the one Gertrude made for Trudy (p. 32) by tying knots and using string. They might make it a "Gertrude doll" by tie-dyeing the handkerchief with colors that they think best represent what Gertrude was like.
3. Have children draw a picture of Edward's thoughts as he sat waiting for his mother to call his name.

Creative Dramatics

1. Let the class pantomime the steps followed by Gertrude in loading the matchlock gun. Have them act out her hurried, worried manner.
2. Pretend it is five years later. Have three children act out a scene in which Edward, now fifteen, tries to convince his uncertain parents to let him join the militia.

Composing

1. Encourage the students to read more about Indian life along the Hudson River in upstate New York during the 1700s: What tribes were present? Were they all warlike? Why did they join with the French? Students should report their findings to the class.
2. Have students write a note that Father Van Alstyne might have sent by Mynderse to his family from Palatine Bridge. What might he have written besides what Mynderse said?
3. Let children imagine themselves as one of the five Indians and describe in a paragraph or two the events that followed

their approach to the Van Alstyne house—from the Indians' point of view.

4. Trudy likes the sound of "Bergom op Zoom," which she says over and over again. Have the children find on a map of New York state (or even Holland) other place names that have interesting sounds. Make a list of these.
5. Have students write a paragraph in which they agree or disagree with one of the following statements.
   a. You should never admit you're afraid.
   b. A ten-year-old child is too young to be given important tasks.
   c. Indians are always to be feared.

Instructional Resources

Record—*The Matchlock Gun*, Miller-Brody Productions (7-NAR 3005), 33 rpm, $6.95.

Cassette—*The Matchlock Gun*, Miller-Brody Productions (7-NAC 3005), $7.95.

Filmstrip (two-part)—*The Matchlock Gun*, Miller-Brody Productions, $32.00 with record (7-NSF 3005) or with cassette (7-NSF 3005-C).

Teaching Guide—"The Matchlock Gun," *A Curriculum for English, Grade 4* (Lincoln: University of Nebraska Press, 1966).

Rabbit Hill

By Robert Lawson. (New York: Viking Press, 1944, 128 pp. Available in paperback from Dell Publishing Co. and Penguin Books.)

Summary

Excitement prevails in the animal community of Rabbit Hill as all the inhabitants, anticipating the arrival of the new owners of the Big House, echo Little Georgie's cry of "New Folks coming." Various adventures related to the arrival take place, especially Little Georgie's exciting trip to get cantankerous Uncle Analdas, Willie Fieldmouse's rescue from a rainbarrel, and Georgie's ominous disappearance. The concern of the New Folks for the animals finally wins them over and results in a community of mutual trust, love, and care. Themes: love of animals, community, change.

Appraisal

Since its publication, *Rabbit Hill* has served as something of a transition between picture books and longer animal fantasies like E. B. White's *Charlotte's Web*. Robert Lawson's effectively shaded drawings, the memorable animal characters, and the satisfying themes contribute to the book's popularity, especially among nine and ten-year-old readers. It won the Newbery Medal in 1945.

Reading Considerations

Assuming a probable audience of third and fourth graders, this book is extremely advanced in vocabulary. Three and four-syllable words are common—*auspicious, ecstatic, indolent, impertinent, lethargy, ultimatum*—but most are used only once or twice. Obviously *Rabbit Hill* must be read to most children, and most of the advanced words should simply be glossed over. Significant, frequently used words (particularly *considerate, approval, speculation, bountiful, frantic,* and *suspicious*) might be discussed before they are encountered in the text.

Initiating Activities

1. Read again *The Tale of Peter Rabbit* by Beatrix Potter. Let the children discuss the kind of people that the rabbits might have preferred to live near instead of Mr. McGregor.
2. Have the class make a list of things they would want to know if they were anticipating the arrival of a new teacher.

Discussion Questions

*1. Do Mother Rabbit and Father Rabbit seem different to you? In what ways? How do they differ in their reaction to the news of "New Folks coming"? How does Father Rabbit talk? Do you know people who talk this way? Do you like to hear them talk? Why or why not?
 2. Why does Red Buck ask Phewie to move around while they talk?
 3. What do some of the animals seem to expect from the New Folks? Do you think they expect too much? Why or why not?
*4. What does Father Rabbit believe about rearing children? Do you agree? Why or why not?
*5. What important job is given to Little Georgie? How does he feel about it? Is too much expected of him? Have your parents ever asked you to do something important? As important as this? How did you feel about it?
*6. What is Uncle Analdas like? Why does he tell Little Georgie he has lost his spectacles? Does he like Little Georgie's song? What sense does he see in it?
 7. How do the various animals feel about Porkey the Woodchuck? If necessary, how do they plan to force him to move? Do you think this is fair? Is Porkey too stubborn?
*8. Of all the animals, which is the most stubborn?
 9. Why do the animals seem happy with the New Folks at first? What does Father Rabbit mean when he says that good manners and good garbage go hand in hand? Why do the workers have trouble understanding the New Folks? How do their feelings toward the animals differ?

10. On Dividing Night, how are the portions decided? Do you think this is a good way to handle it? Why or why not? What other ways might have been tried?
11. Why does Georgie's accident particularly upset the animals? What is it that Porkey tries to tell Mrs. Rabbit at the end of Chapter 10?
*12. Uncle Analdas often seems to cause problems—as with the rumors following Georgie's accident. Why do the other animals put up with him? Would you have been so understanding?
13. In the last chapter, why does Red Buck declare that the garden is forbidden ground?

Art and Media

1. Using Chapter 3 as a guide, have children draw a map of the countryside that Little Georgie followed in his journey from Rabbit Hill to Danbury.
2. The illustration on page 32 shows a "still life" picture in Little Georgie's home. Have children draw some other pictures that might be found in the home, based on the rabbits' backgrounds, habits, and so on.
3. Have the class create a collage around the idea that "there is enough for all."
4. Using "how to" books from the library, help students build a bird and animal feeder to be used on school grounds. A clay model of St. Francis might even be included in the design.

Creative Dramatics

1. Have children act out what might have happened if, in the last chapter, one of the other animals (for example, Porkey or Uncle Analdas) *had* disputed Red Buck's command that the garden not be disturbed.
2. The Mole frequently asks Willie Fieldmouse to "be my eyes." Play a game in which one child (Willie) helps direct a blindfolded student (the Mole) through an obstacle course of chairs, desks, etc. representing the traps or snares.
3. Let two children act out an imaginary conversation between Mother and Father Rabbit about whether or not Little Georgie should continue to visit with the New Folks in their house after his safe return.

Composing

1. Select a volunteer to read in reference books about St. Francis of Assisi and report his or her findings to the class. Was he an actual person? When and where did he live? What is he remembered for?
2. Have the students write a story about how Uncle Analdas might have gotten his ears torn (see the drawing, p. 48).
3. Let students make a list of insults that might have made Mr. Muldoon angry.
4. Suggest that several children write and present to the class a conversation among Uncle Analdas, Mother, and Father about the question of being neat and clean.

Miscellaneous

Since Father Rabbit prefers long words (a typical statement: "This news of Georgie's may promise the approach of a more felicitous and bountiful era"), he might be used as a means of introducing—by tape recorder in a dignified rabbity voice—new vocabulary words each week. The words should be appropriate for the children, of course, and not limited to those in the book.

Instructional Resources

Record—*Rabbit Hill*, Miller-Brody Productions (7-VRB 105), 33 rpm, $6.95.

Cassette—*Rabbit Hill*, Miller-Brody Productions (7-VRB 105-C), $7.95.

Film—*Rabbit Hill*, NBC-TV, 53 minutes, live animals, color; distributed by Contemporary Films (#672347), $610.00 (sale), $40.00 (rental). Narrated by Burl Ives.

Teaching Guide—Charles F. Reasoner, "Rabbit Hill," *Where the Readers Are* (New York: Dell Publishing Co., 1972), pp. 44-50.

Charlotte's Web

By E. B. White. Illustrated by Garth Williams. (New York: Harper
& Row, Publishers, 1952, 184 pp. Available in paperback from
Harper & Row.)

Summary

Wilbur, a runt pig rescued from early death by eight-year-old Fern
Arable, is saved from winter slaughter by his clever and charming
friend Charlotte, a spider who spins words in her web describing
Wilbur as "terrific" and "radiant." The center of adult attention,
Wilbur survives. With her many tasks fulfilled, however, Charlotte
dies. She leaves behind an egg sac of spider children which Wilbur
watches through winter and into spring, when it opens and life is
renewed. Themes: maturity, the acceptance of death and renewal
of life, friendship and loyalty.

Appraisal

This is a modern classic—a good story with memorable characters,
a skillful blending of fantasy and reality, significant themes, humor,
and a beautiful style. E. B. White's text is effectively complemented
by the illustrations of Garth Williams. Invariably popular with
children, *Charlotte's Web* is often taught in the fourth grade.

Reading Considerations

Because of its humor and its many lyrical passages of description,
Charlotte's Web is often read aloud by teachers who recognize its
special values. Some fourth graders can read it independently, but
the book contains numerous advanced words, many of which are
spoken and explained by Charlotte herself. Important words
include *injustice* (pp. 3, 5), *appetite* (7, 12, 111), *commotion* (18,
153), *salutations* (35, 180), *detest* (38, 48), *vaguely* (53, 63, 106),

wondrous (82, 83, 96), *radiant* (99, 100, 101, 114, 120, 121), and *humble* (140, 141, 151).

Initiating Activities

1. Act out a situation in which you have been told by your parents that you must give up your one-year-old pet dog because of several uncontrollable habits, especially barking at night and raiding neighbors' garbage cans.
2. With the teacher's help, design a book called "Friendship Is . . ." in which every student contributes by completing the sentence as he or she wishes ("Friendship is passing notes in class," "Friendship is breaking your Popsicle carefully in half," etc.).
3. Make a list of words that you think of in connection with pigs, spiders, and rats. Keep the list to refer to as you read the book.

Discussion Questions

1. Why is Mr. Arable going out with his ax? What does Fern do when she learns of her father's plans? What else might she have done? What would you do if something like this happened to you?
2. In what ways does Fern treat Wilbur like a baby? Like all babies, Wilbur begins to grow. How and why is Wilbur then moved to a new home?
3. Why is Wilbur unhappy in his new home? When at last he finds a way to escape, Wilbur is still not happy. Describe the ways the following people and animals feel about Wilbur's escape: Mr. and Mrs. Zuckerman and Lurvy; the sheep, the gander, and the cows; Wilbur himself. Can you think of something you wanted to have very much but which disappointed you when you got it?
*4. Wilbur is lonely, but he eventually finds a friend, Charlotte. What does Wilbur dislike about her at first? Why does he grow to like Charlotte better and better?
5. What bad news does the sheep give Wilbur? Who offers to save Wilbur? Does it seem possible to you that a tiny spider could save a pig? Why or why not?
*6. Why is Fern's mother worried when Fern reports the happenings of the barnyard to her? Do you think she should have

been worried? Why or why not? Do you believe that animals can talk? What talking animals have you read about?

*7. Why does Wilbur want to spin a web? Why is he unable to do it? Can you think of times when people are like Wilbur, trying things they know are impossible because they want to show off?

8. How does the goose's unhatched egg save Charlotte? How does Charlotte save Wilbur? What changes does Charlotte's incredible web bring about in the Zuckerman household?

9. Why does Charlotte call a meeting of the animals? What is Templeton's part in the plan? What slogans from ads do you think might be appropriate for Wilbur?

*10. Why does Mrs. Arable go to visit Dr. Dorian? What is his advice to her? Do you think you would like to have Dr. Dorian as your doctor? Why or why not?

11. How is Wilbur prepared for his trip to the fair? Why does Charlotte decide that she and Templeton should go with him?

12. Charlotte has two jobs to complete at the county fair. What are they? What clues can you find that suggest that Charlotte is not her normal self?

*13. During the months that have passed, how has Fern changed? Does her spending less and less time with Wilbur disturb you?

14. Why is Wilbur awarded a special prize at the fair? How does Wilbur react to this award? How does Mr. Zuckerman react?

*15. How does Wilbur repay Charlotte for her friendship and help? Even though Templeton helped Wilbur, too, why was he not such a good friend as Charlotte? What are some of Templeton's virtues?

Art and Media

1. Design and construct a web out of string, yarn, or other material. Place it conspicuously in a corner of the classroom. During the class involvement with the book, the web can be used as a setting for vocabulary words to be learned.

2. Construct a collage that Templeton might have made from food scraps and papers he collected that he would like to hang on his wall.

3. Read the first paragraph in Chapter 6 and paint a watercolor of this or a similar scene.

4. Draw a mural that depicts the passage of the seasons in *Charlotte's Web* and the growth of Wilbur from a runt pig to maturity.
5. Visit a farm and take pictures of various animals that appear in the book, especially pigs, sheep, geese, and spiders. After the prints have been developed, use them to design a box movie with large rollers of a scene from the book.

Creative Dramatics

1. Act out what might have happened if Lurvy and the Zuckermans had seen written in Charlotte's web the words "Swift's Premium Bacon." Improvise their conversation.
2. In pairs, practice looking terrific, then radiant, and finally humble.
3. With several other students, plan and perform a pantomime of Wilbur trying to spin a web (Chapter 9) or Wilbur trying to escape from Lurvy and the Zuckermans (Chapter 3).
4. Act out the conversation between Fern and Mrs. Arable about the animals in the barnyard. The first time, do the scene as it appears in the book. The second time, have Mrs. Arable react in a different manner—angry, disgusted, or sad.

Composing

1. In Chapter 13, Charlotte describes how she goes about writing the word *terrific* in her web. Read in an encyclopedia or some other reference book more about spiders and the spinning of webs. Then write a paraphrase of the account.
2. If possible, spend an hour or so carefully observing a spider in its web. Take notes on its habits, appearance, and prey and report to the class.
3. Write an epitaph for Charlotte.
4. On page 173, Avery says that "coasting is the most fun there is." Fern says it's being in the topmost car of the Ferris wheel with Henry Fussy. Make a list of what Wilbur, Charlotte, Templeton, Lurvy, or Mrs. Arable might have said is "the most fun there is." Add your own statement.
5. Write an account of the strange event involving the spider web on Zuckerman's farm as it might have appeared in a local newspaper.

6. Compile a booklet called "Bits of Wisdom from *Charlotte's Web*." Include statements like "An hour of freedom is worth a barrel of slops."
7. After reading the novel, add to the "Friendship Is . . ." book (see Initiating Activity #2) according to whatever new discoveries you may have made about friendship.

Instructional Resources

Record—*Charlotte's Web*, Miller-Brody Productions (7-Q 1043), 33 rpm, $27.50 for a set of four records. Read by E. B. White.

Cassette—*Charlotte's Web*, Miller-Brody Productions (7-LL DEK9-0089), $79.50 for ten cassettes. Read by E. B. White.

Feature Film—*Charlotte's Web*, Paramount Pictures, 1972; 90 minutes, animated, color; distributed by Films Inc., $75.00 (rental). Directed by Charles A. Nichols and Iwao Takamoto.

Teaching Guide—"Charlotte's Web," *A Curriculum for English, Grade 4* (Lincoln: University of Nebraska Press, 1966).

Teaching Guide—Charles F. Reasoner, "Charlotte's Web," *Releasing Children to Literature* (New York: Dell Publishing Co., 1968), pp. 194-203.

Little House in the Big Woods

By Laura Ingalls Wilder. Illustrated by Garth Williams. (New York: Harper & Row, Publishers, 1932, 238 pp. Available in paperback from Harper & Row.)

Summary

Laura Ingalls and her family live in a gray, log house in the Big Woods of Wisconsin in the 1870s. Throughout the book, she, her mother and father and two sisters work and play together, cheerfully facing the hardships of pioneer life. This book portrays a close family relationship which allows the Ingalls to survive many difficult situations with courage and determination. Themes: family life, security, pioneering in America.

Appraisal

This book by Laura Ingalls Wilder is the first in the series commonly known as the "Little House Books." While this book and its companion volumes have long been popular with children eight to ten years old, a renewed interest has recently been created as a result of the television series about the family, "Little House on the Prairie." This book is a detailed, accurate picture of pioneer life, sprinkled with some fine tales told by Pa. Young readers will find here a portrayal that emphasizes the warm, secure life of a family held together by strong ties.

Reading Considerations

While this book is generally read by children in the intermediate grades, its simple syntactic structures and easy vocabulary make it suitable for younger children who read well. Because of the interesting subject matter, it can also be used with less capable readers in the middle and junior high schools. Important words include *brindle* (p. 3), *curlicues* (61), *catechism* (89, 95), *eaves* (117), *rennet* (187), and *whey* (191).

Initiating Activities

1. Read Aesop's fable, "The Ant and the Grasshopper." How do you and your family prepare for winter? How would you have to prepare if there were no grocery stores? Make a list of the things you would have to grow or make.
2. Try an experiment in cooperation. Design a simple machine made of items found in the classroom such as rulers, pencils, erasers, and paper. See how fast each person can put the machine together. Now try putting it together with each person performing a few jobs which he or she can do well and quickly. Record the amount of time it takes to put the machine together singly and as a group.

Discussion Questions

1. Why is Laura afraid of the wolves in the Big Woods? Have you ever been afraid of some animals that might hurt you? What did your parents say or do to make you feel safe?
2. In the Big Woods, nothing is wasted. When the pig is butchered, everything is used. Tell how each of the following parts is used: (a) body, (b) head, (c) bits and pieces, (d) bladder, (e) tail, (f) bones, and (g) fat.
3. Laura and Mary seem to like to be frightened. They like to hear scary stories and play mad dog with their father. Do you think most children their ages like to be frightened? Why or why not? Discuss some popular television and movie characters and stories that are frightening.
4. What might have happened if Pa had not taken such good care of his gun?
5. How is the Ingalls' Christmas like similar holidays in your house? How is it different? Which is happier, theirs or yours? Why?
*6. Why do Laura and Mary hate Sundays? Why does Pa tell the girls the story about their grandpa's troubles on Sunday? Tell about a time when you were told a story like Pa's that made you feel better. Does it usually make you feel better to know that others share the same or even worse problems? Why or why not?

7. In Chapter 6, what does Laura do when her mother tells her to walk back to the house? Why is she wise to obey her mother so quickly? What might have happened if she hadn't obeyed?

*8. Both Ma and Pa meet "bears" in Chapter 6. Who do you think is braver in these incidents—Ma or Pa? Why? Is a person who faces danger brave, even if the danger is not real? Why or why not?

9. Why is the "sugar snow" such an important happening?

10. Is the dance a special occasion for the members of the Ingalls family? How do you know this? What different things do you do when you are going some place special?

11. Why is Grandma able to outlast Uncle George in the jigging contest? Why does everyone enjoy the contest so much?

*12. Even though Mary and Laura are sisters, they are quite different. Remember the first day Mary and Laura go to town and list ways these two are different—in the way they look, in the way they behave, and in the way others treat them. Do you think Laura is jealous of Mary? Why or why not?

13. How are evenings during the summer different from evenings during the winter in the Little House? Is the same thing true at your house, or are summer and winter evenings the same?

14. Do you feel that Charlie deserves punishment for the tricks he plays on Pa and Uncle Henry? Why or why not?

*15. Why does Pa have the threshing machine brought in? Pa has to talk the other men into stacking their wheat together and sending for the machine. Why do the men need to be persuaded to do this?

16. In Chapter 13, why doesn't Pa shoot any game during his hunt in the woods? How does Laura feel about his not bringing home fresh meat? How would you feel?

17. Many times the Ingalls family faced hard times and had to do without things which we consider necessities today. What are some of the modern conveniences that they did not have which you have? Do these things make life easier and happier for us today? Why or why not?

Art and Media

1. Read carefully the directions for building a smokehouse out of a tree. Make a scale model of the smokehouse, using cardboard and construction paper or a log and wood chips that you find outdoors.

2. Check the library to find pictures of animal tracks like those Laura and her family saw. Make copies of these tracks with potato prints or in modeling clay. Label these tracks and display them in the classroom.
3. In Chapter 6, Pa is frightened by a stump that looks like a bear. Take a long walk and search for odd-shaped branches and rocks that you think look like animals. Bring some of these into the classroom. Ask your classmates to see if they, too, think these objects look like animals.
4. Draw thimble pictures like the ones Mary and Laura drew on the window pane. Use tempera paint, dip your thimble in, and create drawings on newsprint.
5. Try tie-dyeing, using carrots for color just as Ma did (see Chapter 2). Gather up the material you wish to dye in bunches and fasten them with a rubber band. Put the material in the dye and stir it with a stick. Take the material out, put it in a pan, and place the pan in a sink. Rinse the material with clear water. Cut the rubber band. Hang the material up to drip dry.
6. Cut out paper dolls in the shapes of the Ingalls family. Use these paper dolls as stick puppets to act out some scenes from *Little House in the Big Woods*.
7. Read again the directions for braiding straw in Chapter 12 and try to make placemats by braiding straw as Ma did.

Creative Dramatics

1. With a group of friends, act out some of the games Laura and Mary played with Pa.
2. Pantomime the scene in which Pa fights the tree stump that he thinks is a bear.
3. Find Aesop's story, "The Boy Who Cried Wolf." After one group acts out this story, another group can act out the story of Charlie and the yellow jackets. Compare the two stories.
4. Act out the scene in which Ma discovers a bear in the barn lot. Show what might have happened if Laura hadn't obeyed her mother promptly.

Composing

1. Look again at the words to "Yankee Doodle" on page 37. Write a new verse to fit this tune. You may want to write your song about an incident that happened to the Ingalls family.

2. Read over the following old sayings.
   a. Children should obey their parents.
   b. Dog is man's best friend.
   c. Children should be seen and not heard.
   Write a story for one of these sayings which you feel proves the saying to be true. Then write another story to prove the saying is not always true. Share and discuss your stories with the class.
3. Write recipes and directions for making maple sugar and cheese. Be very specific so that anyone could read your recipes and know exactly what to do.
4. Write a diary that Laura Ingalls might have kept. Include at least ten entries in this diary.

Miscellaneous

1. Find a butter churn or use an electric mixer and try making butter in the way the Ingalls did.
2. Find a copy of the *Laura Ingalls Wilder Songbook*. Practice playing and singing some of the songs found in *Little House in the Big Woods.*

Instructional Resources

Record—*Little House in the Big Woods/Little House on the Prairie,* Miller-Brody Productions (7-NAR 3104/5), 33 rpm, double record album, $13.90.

Cassette—*Little House in the Big Woods/Little House on the Prairie,* Miller-Brody Productions (7-NAC 3104/5), double cassette package, $15.90.

Songbook—Eugenia Garson, comp., *The Laura Ingalls Wilder Songbook: Favorite Songs from the Little House Books*; arranged for piano and guitar by Herbert Haufrecht (New York: Harper & Row, 1968).

Homer Price

By Robert McCloskey. (New York: Viking Press, 1943, 149 pp. Available in paperback from Viking Press.)

Summary

The six tales in this book center on Homer Price, his relatives, and his friends who live in Centerburg, a small midwestern town. Homer's many adventures illustrate his clever, perceptive mind at work while pointing up the foibles and insanities of the adult world. Themes: ingenuity, life in a small town.

Appraisal

In this book, author-illustrator Robert McCloskey created an unbelievably popular work which continues to delight children. The slapstick humor and Homer's clever solutions to problems appeal to young people, while McCloskey's subtle and not-so-subtle attacks on the foibles of human beings amuse adult readers.

Reading Considerations

The uncomplicated syntactic patterns and the absence of unusual or difficult vocabulary words make this book a good independent reading choice for fourth and fifth graders.

Initiating Activities

1. Divide the class into two groups. Ask each group to think up a problem, the solution to which requires clever thinking (e.g., a man is trapped in a well and no rope is available; a piece of furniture cannot be moved into a house because the doorway is too small). Then have each group give its problem to the

other group, whose members will brainstorm ways to solve the problem and select the best solution. After discussion, explain to the students that they will be reading about a boy who was very clever at solving troublesome problems.

2. Draw a picture of a rich man. Share the pictures and describe the details which seem to prove the man is rich. Might such a man who seemed to be rich actually be poor? Explore this idea and then discuss other cases in which appearances may give a false picture. This book contains many examples of wrong impressions that you should look for as you read the stories.

Discussion Questions

"The Case of the Sensational Scent"

1. How does Homer tame Aroma? Do you think he is wise in doing this? Why or why not?
2. How does Aroma help Homer capture the robbers? Why doesn't the sheriff come to help Homer when called?
*3. How would you describe the robbers? What characteristics of the robbers make it easy for Homer to catch them?
4. Why do Homer's father and mother let him keep Aroma?
5. Check the illustrations in this chapter very carefully. Can you find the mistake Robert McCloskey made?

"The Case of the Cosmic Comic"

*1. Who is Super-Duper? What super heroes do you know of who are like Super-Duper? How are they different?
*2. Homer says that all of Super-Duper's stories are the same. Does this seem to be true of the super heroes you know?
3. What does Super-Duper not do that convinces Louis and Freddy that he is a regular man? Have you ever found out that someone wasn't as great or fantastic as you thought they were? How did you feel then?

"The Doughnuts"

1. How does Uncle Ulysses feel about labor-saving devices? How does Aunt Agnes feel about them? How can labor-saving devices be helpful? What problems can they cause?

2. What does Uncle Ulysses ask Homer to do while he is gone?
Is he asking too much of Homer? Why or why not?
*3. How are Mr. Gabby and the lady in the shiny black car alike
and different? You will want to consider how they look, how
they live, and how they handle problems.
4. How do Homer and Mr. Gabby handle their problem when
the doughnut machine keeps on making doughnuts? Can you
think of any other things they might have done?

"Mystery Yarn"

*1. Why is Miss Terwilliger known as a very clever woman? Why
do you think she couldn't make up her mind between Uncle
Telemachus and the sheriff?
2. What is the purpose of the string-unrolling contest? What are
the rules, both announced and unannounced, of the contest?
What does Miss Terwilliger do when she hears of the contest?
3. How does Miss Terwilliger win the string-saving contest? Is it
right for her to cheat in order to win the contest? Should
those who see her cheat tell the judges? Why or why not?

"Nothing New Under the Sun (Hardly)"

1. Why is the stranger such a welcome sight in Centerburg? Who
do people think he might be? What do you think of him?
2. What is the meaning of the expression, "If a man can make a
better mousetrap, the world will beat a path to his door"?
How did Mr. Murphy interpret this saying?

"Wheels of Progress"

1. How does Miss Enders decide to show her appreciation to the
people of Centerburg? How does she feel about Uncle Ulysses'
idea of mass-produced homes?
2. Throughout the building of the homes, Miss Enders feels the
process is simply marvelous. Do you think it is good or bad
for all homes to be made alike? What problems does this
cause in Centerburg?

Art and Media

1. Design and construct a new labor-saving device that Uncle
Ulysses might buy for his lunchroom. Consider such incredible

machines as an automatic sandwich maker, a drink mixer and server, or a super sundae maker. You might use coat hangers, cardboard boxes, or other items you find around your home.

2. Design and make a sandwich board to advertise *Homer Price*. Try to make your ads as appealing as possible so others will want to read the book.
3. Make string pictures to illustrate some of the characters from *Homer Price*. These may be realistic pictures showing how you think the characters looked, or abstract pictures showing the personalities of the characters.

Creative Dramatics

1. Act out the scene in which Homer captures the robbers. You might want to try it several times with the robbers being mean or clever.
2. Make up and act out a Super-Duper story. See pages 35-37 for ideas.
3. Read or reread *Rip Van Winkle*, by Washington Irving, and *The Pied Piper of Hamelin*, by Robert Browning. Act these stories out for the rest of the class. Afterwards discuss how the characters and events in "Nothing New Under the Sun (Hardly)" are like these other two stories.

Composing

1. Write a funny mystery story in which the robbers steal something silly and/or end up getting caught in an unusual way.
2. Create your own super hero or heroine. You may draw a comic strip about him or her, write and illustrate a story about your character, or create a storyboard for a movie or television program.
3. Do a class or school survey on hobbies. Make a chart or graph to show the number of people engaged in a particular hobby. Decide who has the most unusual hobby and interview that person. Ask questions such as: How did you get started? How long have you had this hobby? Why do you like this hobby? Take notes on the interview and write a report of it.
4. Throughout the book, the Sheriff has a tendency toward spoonerisms, i.e., he gets words tangled ("cappy houple, bith the weard"). Choose a short speech or poem and try your

hand at spoonerisms. Present your new version to the class. For example,

Bittle Lo Peep
Has shost her leep
And can't tell where to find them.

Instructional Resources

Record—*Homer Price*, Miller-Brody Productions (7-VRB 104), 33 rpm, $6.95.

Cassette—*Homer Price,* Miller-Brody Productions (7-VRB 104C), $7.95.

Film—*The Case of the Cosmic Comic*, Weston Woods, 28 minutes, live-action, color; $350.00 (sale), $25.00 (rental).

Film—*The Doughnuts,* Weston Woods, 26 minutes, live-action, color; $295.00 (sale), $25.00 (rental).

Article—G. H. Poteet, "Getting to See *Homer Price*: Student-Made Filmstrip," *Audiovisual Instruction* 15 (November 1970), 38-39.

Teaching Guide—"Homer Price," *A Curriculum for English, Grade 4* (Lincoln: University of Nebraska Press, 1966).

From the Mixed-Up Files
of Mrs. Basil E. Frankweiler

By E. L. Konigsburg. (New York: Atheneum Publishers, 1967, 162 pp. Available in paperback from Atheneum Publishers and Dell Publishing Co.)

Summary

When Claudia decides to run away, she does it in style, taking her thrifty younger brother Jaime and fleeing to the comforts of the Metropolitan Museum of Art. Here she encounters the mysterious angel statue and searches diligently to discover its identity. Her investigation leads her to the home of Mrs. Basil E. Frankweiler, former owner of the sculpture. With perseverance and skill, Claudia continues her pursuit and finally uncovers Mrs. Frankweiler's secret. Themes: maturity, perseverance, the importance of adventure.

Appraisal

This book, which won the Newbery Medal in 1968, appeals to fourth, fifth, and sixth graders, who delight in the clever schemes of Claudia and Jaime. Students especially enjoy the novel because in the end the children solve the mystery and return home in triumph.

Reading Considerations

Except for a few terms relating to art and history, the vocabulary used in this book is not difficult. Important words include *complications* (pp. 14, 35), *tyrannies* (15), *mohair* (27), *expenditures* (27), *inconspicuous* (30, 34, 52, 55), *orthopedic* (32), *ornately* (38), *sarcophagus* (44, 53, 162), *Renaissance* (50, 53, 144), *commotion* (53), and *amassed* (60). The sentence structure is straightforward and uncomplicated.

Initiating Activities

1. Have you ever planned to run away from home? How did you intend to get away and where did you plan to stay after you had run away? Make a list of the things you would take with you and tell how each item would be used.
2. Share a secret with a friend, but do not tell anyone else about it. After a day or so, tell several others that you have a secret, but do not tell them what the secret is. Then consider this question: Is it much fun to have a secret if no one else knows about it?

Discussion Questions

*1. Why does Claudia decide to run away from home? Do you think she has good reasons for her decision? Why or why not?
 2. What job does Claudia have on Saturdays? How does she feel about this job? Do you have a regular job like Claudia's? How does Claudia's job provide help for her plans? Has your job ever proved to be unexpectedly helpful? In what ways?
*3. How does Jaime manage to save so much money? Would you say that Jaime is thrifty or stingy? Support your answer by referring to details in the story.
 4. Would you agree that Claudia's plan was a brilliant one? Why or why not?
 5. What plans does Claudia make for their continuing education during their stay at the museum? How does Jaime feel about these plans? What else might they have done during their stay?
 6. Why are Claudia and Jaime surprised that they learn so much in the museum? Do you agree with them that a person can learn a lot outside of school? Why or why not?
*7. Why do you think Claudia is so concerned with the statue of the angel? In what ways does she pursue her interest in the statue?
 8. Why does Claudia consider it important that she and Jaime keep clean? How do they do this? What added benefit does this bathing provide?
 9. How do Claudia and Jaime discover their first clue about the statue? What does Claudia plan to do with this new information? Why is she disappointed in the response it brings?

*10. Why does Claudia decide to go to Farmington rather than home? Why is this decision unlike her? Why, then, does she do it? Is this a wise decision? Why or why not?

*11. What bargain do Claudia and Jaime make with Mrs. Frankweiler? Why do the children agree to this bargain? How are Mrs. Frankweiler and Claudia alike?

*12. How is Claudia a changed person when she returns home? Do you think she found her adventure to be satisfying? Why or why not?

*13. What secret does Mrs. Frankweiler know about Saxonbery and the children? How does this secret help to explain the events at the end of the story?

Art and Media

1. The statue is marked with Michelangelo's special mark. Design a mark or monogram of your own that you might use on a work of art.

2. This book has been made into a full-length motion picture of the same name. Pretend that you are the director of the film. Draw a storyboard (a preliminary sketching-out of proposed shots) for one of the more exciting scenes to show how it might be filmed.

3. Pages 48 and 49 show floor plans of the Metropolitan Museum of Art. Design you own art museum and draw a floor plan. Be detailed and indicate places that might be good for hiding.

Creative Dramatics

1. Enact Claudia and Jaime's search through Mrs. Frankweiler's mixed-up files. Reread pages 142-46 first so you will know how they react to their task and to their discovery.

2. Pantomime Claudia and Jaime's bath in the fountain.

3. Try to move a heavy object in the classroom by yourself—a heavy desk, for example. Then get a friend to help you. (You might also pantomime the two actions.) Afterwards, discuss how this teamwork, like the teamwork of Claudia and Jaime, made you feel less burdened.

4. Improvise a scene in which the children are reunited with their parents. What do they tell them? What would their parents say?

Composing

1. Write the note that Claudia sends to her parents. Remember that the note would have been carefully worded so as not to reveal too much.
2. Research the artworks of Michelangelo and write a report emphasizing the breadth of his talent.
3. Write Claudia and Jaime's adventure as if it were a news story or a feature story for a newspaper. Use correct form for the news story, with the lead paragraph containing the most important information.
4. While staying in the museum, Claudia and Jaime sometimes address each other as "Lady" and "Sir" and use very formal language. Write a conversation between two people who are in a very ordinary situation (having lunch in a cafeteria, riding the bus to school, watching a ball game, etc.) but who choose to talk as if they were royalty.
5. Make a list of tasks which your parents require of you, daily or weekly, such as hanging up your clothes or taking out the trash. Prepare a chart containing the list and three columns, one labeled with your name, one with Claudia's, and one with Jaime's. Now imagine you are away from home without adult supervision. Check each task that you would carry out under these circumstances; check each that Claudia or Jaime would do. (Some tasks may be described in the book; others you must decide for yourself based on what you know about the two characters.) When you have finished, write a short paragraph entitled "I am more like Claudia (more like Jaime) because. . . ."

Instructional Resources

Record—*From the Mixed-up Files of Mrs. Basil E. Frankweiler*, Miller-Brody Productions (7-NAR 3010), 33 rpm, $6.95.
Cassette—*From the Mixed-up Files of Mrs. Basil E. Frankweiler*, Miller-Brody Productions (7-NAC 3010), $7.95.

The Lion, the Witch, and the Wardrobe

By C. S. Lewis. (New York: Macmillan Co., 1950, 154 pp. Available in paperback from Macmillan Co.)

Summary

Four children (Peter, Susan, Edmund, and Lucy), sent to stay in an old house in the English countryside, find a wardrobe that leads into the mysterious land of Narnia. There they become involved in a struggle between the evil White Witch and the good lion Aslan. Helped by various animals and mythological creatures and by Aslan's willingness to sacrifice himself, the children overcome the Witch and become the kings and queens of Narnia for many years before finally returning to the old house, where time has not advanced. Themes: good versus evil, sibling love and loyalty, courage, sacrifice.

Appraisal

A book with definite religious and mythic overtones, *The Lion, the Witch, and the Wardrobe* offers children an exciting fantasy with strong characters involved in an intense conflict. The narrative alone will interest many readers from eight to twelve (and beyond); the themes will challenge the mature student especially.

Reading Considerations

This is a well-written novel with ideas that can challenge readers of all ages. It is not, however, exceptionally difficult in vocabulary or sentence structure. Important words that may cause problems include the following: *spiteful* (pp. 20, 35, 36, 128), *sulking* (22, 35, 91), *inquisitive* (8, 29), *prophesy* (66, 109), *betray* (68, 104), *pavilion* (101ff.), and *renounced* (115).

Initiating Activities

1. Have you ever done or seen anything so unusual that your parents or friends wouldn't believe it had happened? What was it? How did you feel when no one believed you? How did you try to convince them? Discuss this with members of your group or class.
2. Read again one of the familiar fairy tales that contains a witch, such as Grimm's "Snow White" or "Hansel and Gretel." With this story and others in mind, make a list of typical witch characteristics—age, appearance, dress, mannerisms, and so on. Keep the list to refer to later.

Discussion Questions

*1. Why were the children sent to the old house in the country? What do you learn about the four children in the first few pages? How do Peter and Edmund differ?
 2. Why does Lucy enter the wardrobe? Why does she leave the door open? Is it good to be curious like Lucy? Why or why not?
*3. Was Lucy afraid of Mr. Tumnus? Would you have been? After entertaining Lucy, why does Mr. Tumnus begin to cry? How does he prove that he is not a bad faun after all? Why do the other children find it impossible to believe Lucy's story? How do their reactions differ?
*4. In their first visits to Narnia, both Lucy and Edmund receive food and drink. How do their experiences differ? Is Edmund afraid of the Queen? What is she like? How does she feel about him at first? Why does her attitude change? Why do you think she seems so interested in the other children?
*5. Why does Edmund lie about his visit to Narnia? Why is he so cross?
 6. In what way is the Professor helpful to the children?
 7. What mysteriously causes all four children to enter Narnia together? Why don't they turn back?
*8. After meeting the Beavers, the children learn about Aslan (p. 63). How do they feel upon hearing his name? Why? Why does Edmund leave the Beavers' house even though "deep down inside him he really knew that the White Witch was bad and cruel"? How do the other children react to his leaving?

*9. Is Peter always brave? Always loyal? Always kind?

*10. Is Edmund completely bad? What are some of the mistakes that he makes in Chapter 9? Which is the worst mistake?

11. Why are the Beavers and the children so anxious to meet Aslan at the Stone Table? Why do the Beavers consider the children so important? What does the phrase "Aslan is on the move" seem to mean?

12. What presents does Father Christmas give to each of the four children? Which one do you think is the most important present? Why?

13. What specific incident causes Edmund to change his mind about the Witch? What gradually happens during their journey toward the Stone Table? What seems to be the cause of the change?

14. Describe the scene at the open hilltop of the Stone Table. How do the children respond to Aslan? How does Peter reveal to Aslan his kindness?

15. How is Edmund rescued? What is the Deep Magic that the Witch reminds Aslan of? What rights does she claim because of it?

*16. What agreement does Aslan make with the Witch to save Edmund? Why do you think he does this? How do the Witch's helpers react to Aslan on the hilltop (Chapter 14)? How does he react?

17. What enables Aslan to recover? How does the "deeper magic" work?

18. In the final battle against the Witch's forces, how does Edmund become a hero? Why does Lucy think that he should be told of Aslan's sacrifice? Do you agree or disagree? Why?

19. Why does Aslan leave Narnia? In what ways is he wild? Are his ways and deeds like any other real or storybook people you have read about?

20. How do the four children return to the Professor's house? Do you think they will want to return to Narnia?

Art and Media

1. Design a flag appropriate for Narnia under the rule of Peter, Susan, Edmund, and Lucy and the watchful eye of Aslan (a banner is described on p. 101).

2. Using whatever medium you wish (pencil, crayon, ink, etc.), make several sketches of the Witch as each of the following

would picture her: (a) her dwarf, (b) the Beavers, (c) Edmund, at first, (d) Aslan, (e) herself.
3. Using coat-hanger wire, thread, and other materials, make a mobile that represents one of the contrasts in the book, such as good against evil or winter and spring.

Creative Dramatics

1. With several other students, pantomime the scene in which Aslan breathes life back into the statues in the Queen's courtyard. Try to mime the animals' movements as life is slowly restored (note the description of the lion on p. 137).
2. Act out what might have happened if Edmund had encountered Mr. Tumnus instead of the Queen in Chapter 3.
3. Mr. Beaver is afraid of being overheard by agents of the Queen. If he had been afraid to speak in his own house, how could he have pantomimed the following information: (a) that Mr. Tumnus had been caught; (b) that Aslan had returned; (c) that the Queen fears the prophecy of Cair Paravel? Pantomime each one.

Composing

1. Several strange creatures common in myths are mentioned in the book: fauns, centaurs, nymphs, dryads, and others. Read about these in a reference book and report to the students in your class or group.
2. As Lucy tells Edmund on pages 33-34, in Narnia it is "always winter, but it never gets to Christmas." Write a paper about how you would feel if it were always winter where you live or about the things you *like* about winter.
3. Write a letter that Edmund might have written home to his mother after his first encounter with the Queen; then write another letter after his second encounter.
4. "People who have not been in Narnia sometimes think that a thing cannot be good and terrible at the same time." Write a paper about something—an animal, a person, an experience— that seems to be both good and terrible.
5. The Professor believes that "there could be other worlds—all over the place, just around the corner. . . ." Write a brief story about another world that you have visited under strange conditions.

Instructional Resources

Article—M. L. Colbath, "Worlds as They Should Be: Middle Earth, Narnia, and Prydain," *Elementary English* 48 (December 1971), 937-45.

Teaching Guide—"The Lion, the Witch, and the Wardrobe," *A Curriculum for English, Grade 5* (Lincoln: University of Nebraska Press, 1966).

Island of the Blue Dolphins

By Scott O'Dell. (Boston: Houghton Mifflin Co., 1960, 184 pp. Available in paperback from Dell Publishing Co.)

Summary

After most of the members of her tribe are killed by trespassing Aleutians and the rest sail away to the east, the Indian girl Karana is left with her brother Ramo on the Island of the Blue Dolphins. Wild dogs kill the boy, but Karana survives, passing the months and years in seclusion except for her dog Rontu and a brief encounter with a friendly Aleutian girl. She catches abalone, builds a shelter, makes tools, befriends animals, and waits—until a ship finally arrives to take her away to the human companionship she has come to need and want. Themes: survival, courage, loneliness.

Appraisal

Winner of the Newbery Medal for 1961, *Island of the Blue Dolphins* is often a favorite among fourth and fifth-grade girls, who respond to this Robinson Crusoe story of a girl surviving against loneliness, fear, and danger. Boys, too, sometimes read the book, attracted by its emphasis on adventure and endurance. The book is based on an authentic account of an Indian girl who lived on the island from 1835 to 1853.

Reading Considerations

Island of the Blue Dolphins is not a difficult book for upper elementary school children. In keeping with its themes and subject, the vocabulary and sentence structure are simple and restrained. Words that might be taught prior to reading include *league* (pp. 9, 32, 33, 65, 126), *kelp* (4, 15, 16, 31, 39, 45), *forlorn* (40), *reproachfully* (149), and *vanquished* (168).

Initiating Activities

1. Write a paper of several paragraphs describing what it would be like if you woke up one morning and found yourself to be the only person left alive on earth. How would you feel? What would you do? How hard would it be to survive? When you have finished writing, share your paper with other members of your group or class.
2. Are you superstitious? Write a list of superstitions that you and your family have. Compare them later with those of Karana in the book. Do her superstitions seem more—or less—sensible than yours? Why?

Discussion Questions

1. What surprises Karana when her father speaks with the Russian? Why do you think he gives his real name? Why do you think they have two names?
2. Why do the tribesmen of Ghalas-at and the Aleutians watch each other? After the battle, why is life in Ghalas-at so troubled through fall and winter?
3. Why do the survivors of the battle finally leave the island? Why does Karana return? Do you think she acts wisely?
*4. Are Karana and Ramo fearful at first? If so—of what? Why does Ramo like it better? What is he so determined to prove? Do you think he is brave or foolish? Was Karana foolish to let him go off by himself?
*5. Why does Karana leave the village? How does she select her new home? Why does she decide she could never wear the beads she finds in the chest? Why is she afraid to make weapons? What changes her mind?
*6. Why is Karana unafraid of canoeing "to the country that lay toward the east"? Why do the stars make her even less afraid once she begins? Cite some incidents that show that Karana is observant and smart. When the leak develops, why does she not want to turn back? What kind of help do the dolphins provide?
*7. How do Karana's feelings about the island change? Why? How does she decide where she will build her house? What are some of the natural materials she uses? Are girls just as good at this kind of thing as boys?

*8. Is Karana superstitious? How do you know? Is she brave? How do you think you would have reacted if you had been Karana?

9. Why does Karana plan to kill the leader of the dogs? Why does she change her mind and carry "the wounded dog, my enemy," home? In what ways does Rontu become helpful?

10. Why does Karana choose not to interfere in the fight between Rontu and the two wild dogs? Is this wise?

*11. Why does Karana cage the two yellow birds? Of what importance are they to her? What else does she do to bring beauty to her life on the island?

12. How do Karana and Rontu get trapped overnight inside Black Cave? What do they find there? Why does Karana decide never to return?

*13. When Tutok appears, why doesn't Karana use her spear? How do the two become friends? Why does Karana finally accept the necklace of black stones?

*14. Throughout her years on the island, is Karana usually happy or sad? What are some things that cause her to feel one way or the other at times? How do her feelings toward animals change? Why?

*15. At first, why did Karana keep a count of the moons that passed? Why does she stop doing this?

*16. Why is Karana so anxious to catch a new dog after Rontu dies?

*17. When the ship appears in Coral Cove, why does Karana try to get the attention of its crew? Do you think she is completely happy about leaving the island at the end? Why or why not? What aspect of life on the island do you think she will miss the most?

Art and Media

1. Design (and perhaps make) a gift that Karana might have made in preparation for her introduction to Father Gonzales at Mission Santa Barbara. The gift should be made of natural materials and should express in some way Karana's feelings about the Island of the Blue Dolphins.

2. Make a time-line that Karana might have kept to remind herself of the important events during her life on the island. You might draw designs on a strip of leather or cloth; or you might

tie bits of cloth or string onto a long length of rope to represent the events.

3. Using an atlas of Southern California (and perhaps the cover of the Dell paperback edition), draw a map of the island. Locate the settings of the book's most important events.

Creative Dramatics

1. Act out a conversation between Karana and Tutok in which Karana tells her friend about the earlier battle between the Aleutians and her tribesmen. (Words may be used occasionally, but the communication should be largely pantomimed.)
2. Pretend that Karana could speak English. Improvise a dialogue between her and the man in the gray robe if she had refused to wear the blue dress.
3. At the end of the book, one of the three men communicates by drawing pictures in the air. Draw the pictures that Karana might have used in her efforts to tell the men and, later, Father Gonzales about her years on the island.
4. After reading pages 136-43 again, pantomime the first two meetings of Karana and Tutok. Try to express the gradual change from fear to trust.

Composing

1. Write a dialogue between the two gods, Tumaiyowit and Mukat (p. 75), discussing the fate of Karana.
2. Read about and write a brief report on one of the following topics: (a) sea otters; (b) abalone or devilfish; (c) tidal waves; (d) the present status of San Nicolas Island, the Island of the Blue Dolphins.
3. Write several pages of a diary that Karana might have kept during her first few days on the island after Ramo was killed and later during the days following Tutok's departure.
4. Among the many objects that Karana makes—several of which are mentioned in Chapter 12—are a bow and arrow. Try to make this weapon yourself; then write directions for constructing it.
5. Ask your classmates to make up two secret names for themselves—one a "real" name common to other people, and the

other a beautiful name (perhaps an Indian name like Won-a-pa-lei) that has an appealing sound. Make a list of the names and share them with the class, keeping the identities of their "owners" secret if the students wish.

Instructional Resources

Feature Film—*Island of the Blue Dolphins,* Universal-International, 1964, 93 minutes, color; distributed by Universal/16 (#26419), $52.50 (rental). Directed by James B. Clark.

Article—R. Wald, "Realism in Children's Literature: *Island of the Blue Dolphins,*" *Language Arts* 52 (October 1975), 938-41.

Teaching Guide—"Island of the Blue Dolphins," *A Curriculum for English, Grade 5* (Lincoln: University of Nebraska Press, 1966).

Teaching Guide—Charles F. Reasoner, "Island of the Blue Dolphins," *When Children Read* (New York: Dell Publishing Co., 1975), pp. 224-233.

Call It Courage

By Armstrong Sperry. (New York: Macmillan Co., 1940, 95 pp. Available in paperback from Macmillan Co.)

Summary

Mafatu is a twelve-year-old Polynesian boy who is afraid of the sea. To escape the taunts of his friends and elders, he sets forth in an outrigger canoe with his dog Vri to prove himself. Enduring a hurricane and loss of his supplies, Mafatu finds a strange, mountainous island and survives for several weeks. During that time he builds a shelter and a new canoe, kills a wild pig and a hammerhead shark, and overcomes his fear of the sea. Finally he escapes the island and a tribe of cannibals, sailing uncertainly until he finds the island of his people, who welcome him as Mafatu, Stout Heart. Themes: courage, survival.

Appraisal

Call It Courage won the 1940 Newbery Award. It is the classic initiation story, simple in plot and theme, powerful and beautiful in style, in harmony with the rhythms and values of Polynesian life. The pen-and-ink drawings by the author are effective. The book will particularly appeal to boys in grades four through seven.

Reading Considerations

A short book, *Call It Courage* seems average in difficulty for upper elementary school students. The plot and sentence structure are not involved; but the vocabulary is frequently advanced, as evidenced by the following list of important words: *indifference* (p. 8), *involuntary* (31, 46, 48), *implement* (52, 56), *lagoon* (19, 23, 41, 59, 52, 54), *ominous* (22, 81), *irresolute* (46, 48), *inevitable* (53), *defiance* (93), and *chaos* (27).

Initiating Activities

1. Most people have had experiences when they felt they were being criticized by their friends. Try to recall an experience like this from your past. In your journal, write about what the friends said, why they were critical, whether or not the criticism was justified, how you felt, and what you did about it.
2. With several other students, compile a group booklet entitled "Courage Is . . ." using the pattern of Charles Schulz's *Happiness Is a Warm Puppy*. Include as many definitions as you can. Examples: Courage Is . . . going to the dentist by yourself . . . admitting that you did something wrong . . . etc.

Discussion Questions

*1. Why do the Polynesians worship courage? Why is it so important to them? Is courage this important to you? Why or why not?
*2. Why is Mafatu afraid? Why does he try to help Kivi, the albatross? Why does he wish he could be like Kivi?
 3. Why does Mafatu leave? Do you think you would have made this choice? Why or why not?
 4. What does Mafatu think about during his first day at sea? As the storm approaches, how does he reassure himself? How does he endure the terrifying storm? How do his companions help? What enables him to struggle toward land after the canoe crashes on the barrier reef? Is this courage? In what way?
*5. Immediately after he awakens, how does Mafatu reveal that he is sensible and mature? How is the new island different from his home? What does Mafatu seem to fear about the island? How does he show himself to be generally less fearful than before?
 6. Besides the man-eaters, what most concerns Mafatu?
*7. How does Mafatu feel about the shark? Why do his feelings change after he makes a knife? What enables him to overcome his fear and kill the shark?
*8. Why is the killing of the wild pig so important to Mafatu? Do you think it was more (or less) important than killing the shark? Why? When Mafatu drags the dead octopus aboard the canoe, why does he plunge the spear again and again into

its body? Is Mafatu afraid when he kills any or all of these enemies?
*9. What does Mafatu learn that courage is?
10. Why does Mafatu feel compelled to see the Sacred Place when he hears the drums?
11. How does Mafatu reveal his final, total victory over Moano, the Sea God?
*12. At the end, Mafatu collapses in his father's arms. Complete his statement.

Art and Media

1. Mafatu is proud of his accomplishments. Use natural materials like those he found (shells, pieces of bone, leaves, twigs, stones, etc.) to design a collage that he might have made to commemorate what he had achieved. Or design a shield or coat-of-arms with figures and symbols that represent each of Mafatu's major triumphs.
2. Draw or paint a picture of the small boat as Kivi might have seen it flying high above (in the first stage of Mafatu's journey). Consider the title "Alone" for your picture, and try to compose it so that it communicates how Mafatu felt in the early part of Chapter 2.
3. Using clay, papier-mâché, or another medium, create masks to represent the qualities that either the Polynesians or the man-eaters would seem to admire the most.
4. Using special 35mm strips of film (one such product is called U-Film, available from Hudson Photographic Industries), black or colored pens, and other materials, create a filmstrip about the storm that Mafatu survives before reaching the sacred island. Also try to find an appropriate musical background for the filmstrip. Show it to the class.
5. Draw two pictures of Mafatu—one as you think he would have drawn himself *before* his adventures, the other as he would have *after* his adventures.

Creative Dramatics

1. With other students, act out the conversation that the Old Ones (p. 18) might have had upon learning of Mafatu's disappearance and, later, when he returned.

2. Mafatu leaves his homeland determined, but uncertain. With another student, act out the two voices speaking within him— the Voice of Determination and the Voice of Fear.
3. Imagine that Mafatu eventually succeeds his father as the Great Chief of Hikueru and one day learns of a young boy who fears the sea as once he did. Enact a scene in which Mafatu speaks with the boy and his parents.
4. Decide as a class some of the important emotions that Mafatu felt through the book (fear, shame, resentment, determination, pride, and others). Then pantomime these emotions, moving from one to the next at intervals signaled by a leader. Concentrate on Mafatu's experiences and intense feelings as he gradually grows from cowardice to courage.

Composing

1. Throughout the book, Mafatu converses with Moano, the Sea God (who opposes him), and Maui, God of the Fishermen (who protects him). Write a dialogue between these two gods during Mafatu's return voyage to his homeland.
2. Write some lyrics for the chant about Mafatu that "the people of Hikueru still sing . . . over the evening fires."
3. Make a dictionary of Polynesian words used in the book, such as *parau, pareu,* and *fei* (they are usually in italics). In some cases, the meaning of the word is given; in others, you will have to determine the meaning from the context.
4. With perhaps a scout handbook as a guide, try building a fire by rubbing two sticks together. Write a report on your efforts and results. Did you succeed? Why or why not? Was it as hard as it was for Mafatu?
5. *Call It Courage* is about Polynesians—their beliefs and customs, their way of life. In encyclopedias, library books, or back issues of the *National Geographic,* find out more about the people of the South Sea Islands and report to the class.
6. After Mafatu removed the spearhead from the base of the idol, "he knew that he had won a great victory over himself. He had forced himself to do something that he dreaded, something that took every ounce of his will" (p. 50). Write about a time when you won a victory over yourself. Compare it to Mafatu's.
7. Suppose there had been no material on the island from which to build a boat. How might Mafatu have communicated with

the people from his homeland? Write a paper offering possible solutions to this problem.
8. Choose one of the following statements and write a paragraph telling why you agree or disagree with it.
    a. Mafatu's fear of the sea was completely justified.
    b. The Polynesians place too much emphasis on courage.
    c. It was foolish for Mafatu to climb to the high plateau after hearing the drums.
    d. Mafatu's triumphs over the shark, the pig, and the octopus are too hard to believe.

Instructional Resources

Record—*Call It Courage*, Miller-Brody Productions (7-NAR 3002), 33 rpm, $6.95.
Cassette—*Call It Courage,* Miller-Brody Productions (7-NAC 3002), $7.95.
Filmstrip (two-part)—*Call It Courage*, Miller-Brody Productions, $32.00 with above record (7-NSF 3002) or with above cassette (7-NSF 3002-C).
Teaching Guide—Charlotte S. Huck, *Children's Literature in the Elementary School*, 3rd ed. (New York: Holt, Rinehart and Winston, 1976), pp. 724-25, 734-35.

Old Yeller

By Fred Gipson. (New York: Harper & Row, Publishers, 1956, 117 pp. Available in paperback from Harper & Row.)

Summary

When his father leaves for a cattle drive, Travis Coates remains to help his mother tend their frontier Texas farm. A big, rangy yellow dog appears, and over the summer Travis and Old Yeller experience one adventure after another. The book culminates in Old Yeller's battle with a rabid wolf, after which the boy is forced to carry out his heaviest responsibility—shooting the dog he has grown to love. Themes: responsibility, courage.

Appraisal

Set in the late 1860s, *Old Yeller* has been a favorite among children of ten to twelve for twenty years. A brisk plot, the authentic flavor of frontier Texas hill country, the emphasis upon a young boy assuming responsibility, and one of the more memorable dogs of children's literature—these elements and others insure the book's continued popularity.

Reading Considerations

Old Yeller is narrated by the main character remembering himself as a fourteen-year-old boy in backwoods Texas, and its vocabulary and sentence structure are not difficult. The few difficult words include *depredation* (p. 4), *careen* (30), *poultice* (34, 90, 96), and *hydrophobia* (46ff.)

Initiating Activities

1. Along with your classmates, bring to school a picture of a dog that was (or is) very important to you. In a paragraph describe the dog and how he was a friend and helper. Compile the pictures and paragraphs into a class book or collage.
2. Conduct a survey: ask your friends and classmates what jobs they are responsible for at home, what they do to earn money, and so on. Find out if they perform any tasks that are usually done by adults or any that are in some way dangerous. Also ask them what older brothers and sisters do. Report your findings to the class.

Discussion Questions

1. Why does Travis's father leave his family for several months? What does he expect of Travis? Do you think that his expectations are unreasonable? Why or why not? How does Travis respond? How might you have responded?
2. Why is Travis not interested in dogs at the beginning of the book? Why doesn't he like Old Yeller? What incident changes his opinion?
*3. How does Travis feel about Arliss? Why does Arliss sometimes make him angry? Why do you think Travis loves Arliss "maybe in some ways even a little bit more" than he loves his parents?
4. Travis sometimes refers to Old Yeller as a rascal or rogue. In what ways is this accurate?
5. What is a "suck-egg dog"? How do Travis and his mother find out that Old Yeller has become one?
*6. Why doesn't Travis respect Bud Searcy? Does he also dislike or even hate him? Is it possible to like someone and not respect him? Can a person be respected and not liked?
7. In what ways does Old Yeller help the family besides protecting them from wild animals?
*8. Why do you think Burn Sanderson lets Travis and Arliss keep Old Yeller? Why does he tell Travis and not Mama about the hydrophobia?
*9. Why does Travis enjoy rounding up and marking hogs? How does his working with the hogs reveal that he has courage?

*10. What are some of the ways the dramatic fight with the hogs reveals the love between Travis and Old Yeller? Was it smart for Travis to return to the wounded dog? Was it right? Are there times when you have to do what's right even though it may not be wise? Can you think of examples?

*11. Discuss two or three incidents in Chapter 12 that show the sensitivity of the characters to the feelings and needs of others.

12. Why do Travis and Mama refuse to admit to themselves that the heifer Spot has hydrophobia?

13. Why do you think Old Yeller accompanies Mama and Lisbeth to burn the heifer's carcass? Do you think you would have been able to shoot Old Yeller as Travis does? Can you think of times when you (or your parents) had to do something that hurt you (or them) simply because it had to be done?

*14. Travis's father says, "It's not a thing you can forget. I don't guess it's a thing that you ought to forget." What does he mean?

15. At the end of the book, what—besides the horse—causes Travis to feel alive and happy again?

Art and Media

1. The incident where Travis falls among the wild hogs is terrifying ("I guess I screamed. I don't know. It happened too fast. All I can really remember is the wild heart-stopping scare . . ."). Using oils or finger paints and perhaps pieces of paper or objects, try to depict Travis's feelings during that awful moment. Give your work a one-word title.

2. From information given in the book, draw a map of the area in which Travis lives, including Birdsong Creek, the cabin, the spring, the Salt Licks, and the bat cave country.

3. *Old Yeller* has no illustrations, but pictures of some of the incidents would be helpful. One of these is the scene described in activity #1. Draw a picture of Travis trying to rope the pigs from the lip of the cutbank above them. (Pictures of other scenes by students could be compiled to make a packet of illustrations to go with the book.)

Creative Dramatics

1. With another student, act out a scene between Travis and his mother and father at the end of the book in which Travis

argues that Arliss should not be allowed to keep the speckled pup because of the pain of losing such animals.

2. With three other students, act out the scene where Bud Searcy and Lisbeth visit for the first time. Try to make Bud Searcy seem lazy, newsy, and considerate; Mama, polite but proud; Travis, interested and impatient; and Lisbeth, solemn and wise.

3. Imagine Travis fifteen years later as the father of a small son who asks him to tell about Old Yeller and the wild hogs. Using a recorder, tell the story as Travis might have.

Composing

1. Write a letter that Travis's mother might have written to his father in care of the Abilene mail service, telling about the events up to the hog fight and about how Travis has handled himself.

2. After reading in the *Foxfire* series or in similar books, write an explanation of how to do one of the following frontier tasks mentioned in the book: (a) make lye soap; (b) dress or skin a deer; (c) make a poultice.

3. Write a brief account of what might have happened if Burn Sanderson had not allowed Travis and Arliss to keep Old Yeller.

4. In a reference book, read about hydrophobia—its causes, effects, treatment—and write a brief report. Include information that the Coates family was not sure of: for example, whether or not cattle become rabid and how the disease is spread. Be prepared to give your report to the class.

5. Remembering Arliss's tendency to exaggerate, write a brief description of the bear incident as he might have told it.

Instructional Resources

Record—*Old Yeller,* Miller-Brody Productions (7-NAR 3037), 33 rpm, $6.95.
Cassette—*Old Yeller,* Miller-Brody Productions (7-NAC 3037), $7.95.

The Borrowers

By Mary Norton. (New York: Harcourt, Brace and Co., 1953, 180 pp. Available in paperback from Harcourt Brace Jovanovich.)

Summary

Mrs. May recounts to Kate the tale of the borrowers, those small people who exist under the floor of the house by "borrowing" needed items from the family of the house. Fortunately for the Clock family of borrowers, Arrietty, their daughter, becomes friends with a young boy who is living in the house. When the hateful housekeeper discovers Arrietty and her family and makes plans to exterminate them, this boy helps the Clocks to escape. The reader is left with the impression that the borrowers now are living happily in the field. Themes: the importance of family life, survival.

Appraisal

This book delights both youthful and adult readers as they explore the miniature world of the borrowers, complete to the tiniest detail. While the story is clearly a fantasy, the realistic depiction of characters and situations draws the reader into the world of these little people where they can be accepted as flesh-and-blood characters with real problems.

Reading Considerations

The Borrowers may be read independently by strong readers in the intermediate grades; however, because of the novel situations and the interesting commentary on human life that the book presents, it would be a good choice for reading aloud to children. Challenging vocabulary includes *badger's set* (p. 29), *spinney* (29, 87, 173), *wanly* (40), *contrite* (44), *lintel* (61), *harebell* (72), *flotsam and jetsam* (78), *ferret* (101, 103, 104, 117, 142), *scullery* (21, 104, 139, 140, 141, 155, 168), *imperative* (116), *golliwog* (121), *disheveled* (131), *morose* (161), *wainscot* (12, 43, 163, 164), and *stoats* (174, 175).

Initiating Activities

1. Do you have problems with small objects being lost in your house? Make a list of objects that you often can't find. What do you think happens to these things? List reasons why these things are lost (e.g., being sucked up in a vacuum cleaner, falling behind the couch, etc.). Now compile a list of fantastic reasons why they may be lost (e.g., being picked up and moved by a good fairy or transformed by a witch's spell).

2. Collect five or six small objects from around the classroom, such as a paper clip, a scrap of paper, or a piece of chalk. Imagine that you are only six inches tall and make a chart showing how you might use these things. Keep this chart so you can review it and add to it after you finish reading the book.

Discussion Questions

1. How does Mrs. May find out about the borrowers? Why is her brother able to see things that other people cannot see?

2. Do you think the last names of the borrowers are appropriate? Why or why not? In what other ways might they have chosen their names?

3. How does Homily feel about Pod's adventure in the schoolroom? Why does she feel this way?

4. What has happened to the other borrowers that had lived in the house? Why must Arrietty be told about the fate of the others?

*5. Why does Arrietty want to go borrowing? Why does Pod agree that she should be allowed to do this? Have you, like Arrietty, ever longed for adventure and a chance to see new places, even though you knew such experiences might be dangerous?

6. What strange, unusual things does Arrietty see on her first borrowing trip? What other objects might have appeared strange to a person of Arrietty's size?

*7. What is Arrietty's first reaction to the boy? How does she feel about him after she has talked with him for a while? How do you think you would react in such a situation?

8. The boy and Arrietty disagree about "borrowing." How do you feel about this? Is stealing always wrong? Is taking something that belongs to someone else always stealing? How do the borrowers justify their actions?

*9. Why doesn't Arrietty believe what the boy tells her about the world of "human beans"? Why doesn't the boy believe Arrietty about the world of the borrowers? What plan do they devise to help settle this dispute?

10. Do you believe that Arrietty is wise in sending a note to her uncle? Why or why not? What problems might her actions have caused?

11. How does the boy get into the Clock's house? How do Homily, Pod, and Arrietty feel about his visit? How would you have reacted?

12. How does the boy's borrowing finally lead to trouble? Do you think that most people are like Homily Clock? That is, rather than being content when good things come their way, do they still covet more and more? Why do you think people are like (or not like) this?

*13. What kind of woman is Mrs. Driver? Why does she want to get rid of the borrowers? Why isn't the boy able to prevent Mrs. Driver from carrying out her plan?

*14. Why does the boy make one desperate attempt to save the borrowers? What would you have done in his place?

15. Why does Mrs. May still believe the Clocks are safe and comfortable in the badger's set? What evidence suggests that the borrowers were invented by Mrs. May's brother?

Art and Media

1. Make a piece of furniture for the Clock's house. Use only odds and ends that you find around your own house, such as spools, matchboxes, or other discarded objects.

2. Prepare a mini-museum of objects that might have been used by borrowers. You may use specific items described in the book, but try to find other objects as well. Prepare a card for each object, listing its original use and its use in the borrowers' home.

3. Make two drawings of one room in the Clock's house showing how the room looked before the boy's borrowing and how it looked after the new additions.

Creative Dramatics

1. Act out with your classmates one of the following scenes: (a) Arrietty's first meeting with the boy, (b) the boy's first visit to the Clock's home, (c) Homily and Pod's discussion of Arrietty's sending a letter to Uncle Hendreary.
2. Pantomime the actions of Pod and Arrietty as they go borrowing.
3. Make up and act out a new adventure for the borrowers. You may want to read *The Borrowers Afield* or *The Borrowers Afloat* by the same author to get ideas for this drama.

Composing

1. Choose a scene you know well, such as your classroom or your room at home, and write a description of it as if you were Arrietty. Remember how tall you would be and how things would look to you.
2. Make a menu for the Clocks for one day. List the specific foods and the amounts they would eat for each meal.
3. Write five entries for Arrietty's "Memoranda" book. Remember that Arrietty wrote only brief notes about the important things that happened (see p. 95). Now rewrite each of these entries and make each more complete so the reader will know how Arrietty felt about each experience.
4. Pod and Homily make it clear that they feel that "Parents are right, not children." Make a list of the times you think Arrietty was right and her parents were wrong.

Instructional Resources

Record—*The Borrowers*, Caedmon (TC 1459), 33 rpm, $6.95. Narrated by Claire Bloom.
Cassette—*The Borrowers*, Caedmon (C 1459), $7.95.
Article—B. V. Olson, "Mary Norton and *The Borrowers*," *Elementary English* 47 (February 1970), 185-89.

A Wrinkle in Time

By Madeleine L'Engle. (New York: Farrar, Straus & Giroux, 1962, 211 pp. Available in paperback from Dell Publishing Co.)

Summary

Hoping to rescue her father from a mysterious fate, Meg Murry, along with her precocious brother Charles Wallace and their friend Calvin O'Keefe, travels through time to the planet Camazotz with the assistance of Mrs. Whatsit, Mrs. Who, and Mrs. Which. There they confront IT, the planet's intimidating force for conformity. Helped by her father and several strange but gentle creatures, Meg overcomes frustration and disillusionment, triumphing by using the one power IT cannot comprehend: love. Themes: love, individuality, courage.

Appraisal

A Wrinkle in Time is a challenging, thought-provoking book, beautiful in theme as well as style. Winner of the Newbery Medal in 1963, it has become a sixth-grade standard in many schools. Although it is read by many students independently, the book will bear much discussion.

Reading Considerations

Frequent references to scientific terms (*tesseract, megaparsec*), the religious symbolism, figurative language, and challenging philosophical issues may make this book difficult reading for some students. Important words include *indignant* (pp. 17, 54, 59, 61, 80, 197), *vulnerable* (9, 102, 183, 208), *materialize* (55, 81, 84, 99, 193), *verbalize* (61, 67, 84), *tangible* (71, 99, 152, 211), *aberration* (106), *inexorable* (58, 157, 205), *ominous* (140, 156), *emanate* (143, 176, 191), *fallible* (172, 183), and *omnipotent* (158, 172).

Initiating Activities

1. Imagine a town in which all streets, buildings, and people look alike. All people in this place must behave in a specific way. Regulations are enforced by a strict ruler who severely punishes all who do not conform. Draw a mural of this place or write a description of how the people live.
2. Do you believe in ESP (extrasensory perception) or mental telepathy? What examples of these phenomena have you heard or read about? Try an experiment with a friend: think of a word or phrase, concentrate on it, and see if your friend can "feel" what it is.
3. Pretend that your grades have recently been dropping. With other students, act out a scene in which you react to your teacher's suggestions that the reason for your decline is your father's absence for long periods of time as a traveling salesman.

Discussion Questions

1. What causes Meg's problems in her schoolwork and in her relationships with her teachers and the principal?
*2. Why is Charles Wallace called a special person?
*3. Compare Calvin O'Keefe's mother to Mrs. Murry. Also compare the way Calvin and Meg feel about their mothers. How do you explain the similarities and differences?
4. Mrs. Who and Mrs. Which have problems communicating. Describe their problems and how they try to handle them. Why doesn't Mrs. Whatsit have these problems?
*5. Explain the changes in Meg's attitude toward Mrs. Whatsit. What does Meg think of her when she first meets her? How and why do her feelings change?
*6. With what do you usually associate black and darkness? What does the Black Thing mean to you?
*7. Discuss the possible meanings of IT. What happens when people accept authority without question? Can you think of any times this has happened? Do you know any countries where such a situation exists?
8. Several people are able to resist the powers of IT. What enables Calvin, Meg, Mr. Murry, and finally Charles Wallace to escape IT?

*9. How do Meg's weaknesses become her strengths? Is it ever true that this, too, can happen in everyday life? Can you think of examples of this in your own life?

*10. IT says, "But that's what we have on Camazotz. Complete equality. Everyone exactly alike." To this, Meg replies, "*Like* and *equal* are not the same thing at all." Discuss these two positions. How do they relate to life in our society?

*11. Describe Aunt Beast. Is her appearance consistent with her behavior? Do you often judge people by their appearances? Can you think of times when you have done this and been wrong?

12. Throughout the book, smells are associated with feelings. Think about some particular odors (Mrs. Murry's stew, the fragrance of Uriel, the smell of Aunt Beast) and decide what feelings these are associated with.

*13. Why must Meg be the one to return for Charles Wallace? How would you feel in her position?

Art and Media

1. With rollers, tabs, buttons, etc., design and make a "number one spelling machine" that would show the spellings of words which follow a particular spelling generalization, such as "i" before "e" except after "c" or never a "q" without a "u." Use your machine with younger children to see how well it works.

2. Using pictures, objects, and scraps of materials, create a collage on the idea of fear, love, or anger as reflected in *A Wrinkle in Time*.

3. Design a mobile that illustrates the concept of "a wrinkle in time."

4. Draw a series of cartoons showing Mrs. Whatsit's transition from a funny old lady to a beautiful winged creature. If a movie camera is available, make an animated film of this transformation.

Creative Dramatics

1. In Chapter 9, Meg attempts to counteract the force of IT by quoting nursery rhymes and the Gettysburg Address. To see how difficult this task is, try to decide when a minute has passed while your partner attempts to distract you by engaging you in conversation.

2. Pantomime or enact the coordinated ball bouncing and rope skipping of the Camazotz children, referred to in Chapter 6. How difficult is it? How would you feel if you were made to do this?
3. Meg experiences many strange sensations as she "tesseracts" through time and space. Attempt to recreate these experiences by blindfolding each member of the group and providing a unique variety of stimuli for touching, smelling, and hearing. An electric fan, ice cubes, perfume, etc. may be used. After everyone has a turn, try to pantomime the phenomenon of tesseracting.
4. Improvise what might have happened if, in the last chapter, Charles Wallace had responded to Meg's love by saying, "Love is strongest among those who look and live and act alike."

Composing

1. Think of a highly repulsive creature—perhaps a vulture—and describe ways in which it is beautiful.
2. Imagine you are Charles Wallace under the influence of IT. Write a letter to your mother in which you try to convince her to join you on Camazotz.
3. Write a paragraph in which you describe a sunset to someone who is blind.
4. Write a diary that Calvin might have kept during the journey.
5. Research the idea of tesseracting, i.e., of traveling through time, and report to the class.
6. Compile a booklet of quotations that you might offer to others as examples of humanity's wisdom if you were Mrs. Who.
7. Write a composition entitled "Flatland: Twenty-Four Hours in a Two-Dimensional World."

Miscellaneous

1. Imagine that you are filming this book. Find suitable background music for certain scenes, such as Chapter 4, "The Black Thing." Then present selections from these parts of the book with your selected musical accompaniment.
2. Debate the following statements in your class or group.
   a. It was wrong for Mr. Murry to leave home on such a dangerous mission.

b. Meg should not have talked back to her principal and teacher.
c. Meg was right to blame her father for leaving Charles Wallace.
d. Mrs. Who, Mrs. Which, and Mrs. Whatsit should not have sent Meg, Calvin, and Charles Wallace into Camazotz alone.
e. In our society, you can judge people by their appearance, although you could not do this with the beasts of Ixchel.

Instructional Resources

Record—*A Wrinkle in Time*, Miller-Brody Productions (7-NAR 3033), 33 rpm, $6.95.
Cassette—*A Wrinkle in Time*, Miller-Brody Productions (7-NAC 3033), $7.95.
Filmstrip (two-part)—*A Wrinkle in Time*, Miller-Brody Productions, $32.00 with above record (7-NSF 3033) or with above cassette (7-NSF 3033-C).
Teaching Guide—"A Wrinkle in Time," *A Curriculum for English, Grade 6* (Lincoln: University of Nebraska Press, 1966).
Teaching Guide—Charles F. Reasoner, "A Wrinkle in Time," *When Children Read* (New York: Dell Publishing Co., 1975), pp. 67-78.

Julie of the Wolves

By Jean Craighead George. (New York: Harper & Row, Publishers, 1972, 179 pp. Available in paperback from Harper & Row.)

Summary

Trying to escape an intolerable arranged marriage, a thirteen-year-old Eskimo girl named Miyax (Julie in English) finds herself lost on the Alaskan tundra. Facing hunger and bitter cold, she survives through her own resourcefulness and through her communication with a pack of wolves, who provide food, love, and inspiration. Miyax grows to prefer the wilderness of wolves and her own Eskimo heritage to the trappings of civilization; but she sadly concludes that she cannot escape the latter. Themes: survival, courage, the conflict between nature and civilization, the importance of wild animals and wilderness.

Appraisal

Julie of the Wolves is a compelling story of survival popular with girls and many boys in grades five through seven. Much of its considerable appeal is attributable to the wolves and their relationship with Miyax, to the beautiful but formidable Arctic setting, and to Miyax's developing understanding of how she relates to her heritage and her environment. The book has been criticized for a rape scene, but the incident is handled so discreetly that most children will take little notice. *Julie of the Wolves* won the Newbery Medal for 1973.

Reading Considerations

Because of the flashback in Part II and Miyax's uncertainty at the conclusion of the book, the plot of *Julie of the Wolves* is more demanding than that of most juvenile novels. In addition, the vocabulary would be challenging to many eleven and twelve-year-old readers, with the following important words being typical: *discern* (pp. 6, 125), *regal* (6, 137, 153), *intimidated* (19), *laborious* (30, 45), *deference* (33), *improvise* (53, 126), *reprimand* (61), *deft* (114, 123), and *authoritative* (131, 161). Despite these factors, the book could be read independently by most of the children who find it interesting.

Initiating Activities

1. Find a copy of the record *The Language and Music of the Wolves,* narrated by Robert Redford (Columbia Records, C 30769), perhaps at the public library. Discuss your reactions to the sounds of "wolf music" with other members of your class.
2. If possible, view and discuss a film or filmstrip on the Alaskan tundra. Consider the nature of such an environment and what it would be like to live there. (The National Geographic film *Journey to the High Arctic*, available from many state department of education film libraries, would be excellent for this.)

Discussion Questions

*1. How does Miyax feel about being alone on the tundra among wolves? Is she afraid? How would you have felt in a similar situation?
*2. Do you agree with the Eskimos on Nunivak Island that the riches of life are intelligence, fearlessness, and love? Why or why not? What other qualities might you add?
3. How does Miyax gain Amaroq's acceptance? What evidence does the book give that wolves are intelligent? Kind?
*4. How does Miyax feel about her father Kapugen? How does he help her in her predicament even though he is absent?
5. How is Miyax finally successful in getting meat? How do you feel about the incident? Why do you think Miyax so easily accepts it?
*6. What are Miyax's feelings toward the wolves? Does she respect them or love them or both? Do her feelings change? If so, how? How does she feel toward Amaroq? Toward Kapu? Toward Jello? Do your own feelings toward wolves change as you read the book? If so, how?

*7. As she recalls her childhood (Part II), why did Miyax prefer being called an Eskimo instead of gussak? Why did she not want her father to call her Julie? Why were the two of them so close?

8. What differences between Eskimo life and life in California did Amy's first letter reveal? What did Julie mean by "Daylight is A-M-Y"? Why did she want to go to San Francisco?

9. In what ways was life at Barrow tolerable? Intolerable? How did her father's earlier advice persuade her to leave? Do you agree that fear results when you do something wrong? Why or why not?

*10. In Part III, as Miyax heads toward Point Hope, how does her attitude toward Eskimos change? Why does she feel their accomplishments were equal to "sending rockets to the moon?" Do you agree with her? Why or why not? Why does she become increasingly concerned for the wolves' safety?

11. Why does Miyax dance after Kapu's visit to the tent (p. 126)? Why does she feel the dance has purpose?

*12. When Amaroq is shot, Miyax looks up at the plane and sees "great cities, bridges, radios, schoolbooks . . . the pink room, long highways, TV sets, telephones, and electric lights." What does this mean? Why does she have this vision?

*13. Why does the comb she has carved become so important to Miyax?

*14. Why does Miyax become so excited during the conversation with Uma? Why does she refuse to speak English? Why is she so disappointed when she finds Kapugen? How has he changed?

*15. What does Tornait's death seem to mean to Miyax? At the end, why does she point "her boots toward Kapugen" again? How do you feel about the ending?

*16. What other title might the book have? Why was it not titled *Miyax of the Wolves*? Why not *Julie and the Wolves*?

Art and Media

1. Miyax carves a totem of Amaroq from bone and asks him "to enter the totem and be with her forever." Using wood or soap, carve a totem of your own—of an animal whose qualities or "spirit" you admire and respect.

2. When Miyax recalls the good years at seal camp (pp. 76ff.), she refers to colored memories ("flickering yellow," "a silver memory," etc.). Using colored pencils and watercolors, draw

and paint a favorite memory of hers—or yours—in the appropriate color.

3. With the description on page 5 and the double-page illustration preceding it as guides, paint a mural of the tundra as Miyax sees it in Part I of the book. Take particular care to capture the color of the tundra, using other passages (e.g., p. 9) for information.

Creative Dramatics

1. Act out the conversation between Miyax and Kapugen that will take place after the book ends.
2. In the book the wolves quite obviously communicate with each other. As though they could speak, act out the response of Kapu, Silver, and Nails to Miyax's final command that they not follow her to the village of Kangik.
3. Pantomime how the wolves communicated the following messages.
   a. "I am the leader."
   b. "I surrender."
   c. "I am angry and suspicious. Lie down!"
   d. "We recognize you as our leader."

Composing

1. On page 11, a list of things Miyax thought necessary for survival includes "a backpack, food for a week or so, needles to mend clothes, matches, her sleeping skin and ground cloth to go under it, two knives, and a pot." Imagine yourself in a similar situation. After visiting a local backpacking store, determine what items (no more than ten) you would need for surviving two weeks in the wilderness in, say, October. List your items in a paragraph, explaining why each is important.
2. Write a letter that Miyax might have written to Amy after returning to Kapugen at the end of the book.
3. Write a diamante poem contrasting nature and civilization.[1]
4. Try to observe a dog of your acquaintance over a period of time. Focus on the dog's body language and facial expressions. Jot down notes on how the dog seems to communicate pleas-

---

[1] For a description of this form of poetry, see the guide to *The Hundred Penny Box*, "Composing."

ure, fear, uncertainty, anger, and so on. Write up your observations in a report.

5. Write what you think Amaroq's thoughts might have been from the time he first sees Miyax (p. 11) to the moment she becomes one of the pack (p. 25).
6. In reference books and other works, find out more about wolves—their packs, their ability to communicate, their hunting habits, their present range, and especially their chances of survival. Report your findings to the class.
7. A similar book by Jean George tells how a young boy survives for several months in a wild area in New York State. Read *My Side of the Mountain* and write a brief comparison of it and *Julie of the Wolves.*

Instructional Resources

Record—*Julie of the Wolves,* Miller-Brody Productions (7-NAR 3040), 33 rpm, $6.95.
Cassette—*Julie of the Wolves,* Miller-Brody Productions (7-NAC 3040), $7.95.
Filmstrip (two-part)—*Julie of the Wolves,* Miller-Brody Productions, $32.00 with above record (7-NSF 3040) or with above cassette (7-NSF 3040-C).
Film—*Journey to the High Arctic,* National Geographic Society, 1971, 52 minutes, color; distributed by University of Iowa Media Library, $20.15 (rental).

Are You There God?
It's Me, Margaret

By Judy Blume. (Scarsdale, N. Y.: Bradbury Press, 1970, 149 pp. Available in paperback from Dell Publishing Co.)

Summary

Margaret Simon is nearly twelve, and she is perplexed because she cannot reconcile her personal relationship to God with the formal religious services she attends. She is also troubled because her new friends are anxious about bras and periods, and she feels that she too must adopt these concerns. Eventually these two problems come together and help resolve Margaret's predicament. Themes: growing up, the significance of religion.

Appraisal

Within this lively book, Judy Blume humorously and compassionately portrays the problems of a preadolescent girl seeking an understanding of formal religion while struggling with the uncertainties of peer acceptance and physical development. Although boys would better understand the problems of girls after reading this book, *Are You There God?* is intended for girls, with whom it is immensely popular.

Reading Considerations

Narrated by the main character, this book should not prove difficult for average readers at the fifth, sixth, and seventh grade levels. Important words include *expressly* (pp. 2, 62), *sulked* (40), *rabbi* (60), *Hanukkah* (74, 75), and *abominable* (87). Because of the book's frank discussion of menstruation, many teachers will prefer to use it with small groups.

Initiating Activities

1. If you have ever moved or if you have ever had to change schools, make a list of the problems you experienced. (If you've never moved, try to imagine what the problems would be.) Compare your list with that of a classmate.
2. Discuss the following statements with your classmates.
   a. Parents should tell their children what church to attend.
   b. The most important thing in life is to be accepted by your friends.
   c. The most important thing in life is to make decisions for yourself, regardless of what your friends or parents think.

Discussion Questions

1. Which aspects of Margaret's new home are appealing? Which are not appealing? Why does Margaret feel that her grandmother is responsible for their moving?
*2. What are Margaret's first reactions to Nancy? What do you think of Nancy? Why does Margaret talk to God about her?
3. Why is everyone surprised to see Margaret's grandmother? What arrangements do Margaret and her grandmother make? How does Margaret feel about all the attention her grandmother gives her?
4. The PTS's choose new names for themselves. Which of the names do you think are "sensational"? Why? What "sensational" name would you choose for yourself?
5. Why doesn't Margaret have a religion? Does this bother her? What does she decide to do about it? What other actions might she have taken?
6. What pranks do the students play on Mr. Benedict? Do you think he handles these problems well? Why or why not?
*7. Discuss Margaret's experiences with formal religious services. Why do you think they are so unsatisfactory?
*8. Throughout the book Margaret and her friends are worried about maturing physically. Why is this so important in their lives at this particular time? Do you think they are overly concerned about these matters? Why or why not?
*9. What good things happen to Margaret on her twelfth birthday? What rotten things happen? Do you think she takes some of the unpleasant things too seriously? Why or why not?

*10. How and why does Margaret's attitude toward Laura Danker change? Do you feel Laura has been treated unfairly by her classmates? Why or why not?

*11. How does Margaret's experience with her grandparents turn her against religion? Do you think that both sets of grandparents treated Margaret unfairly? Why or why not?

*12. What happens to bring Margaret back to God? What evidence do you find to show that Margaret is growing up?

*13. Throughout the book Margaret and her friends try very hard to be alike. Do you think this is harmful or helpful or both? In what ways?

Art and Media

1. Make a collage showing people, clothes, and objects that are important in the life of a twelve-year-old girl.

2. Draw a picture of a pre-teen girl who is a "sensational" dresser. Compare your picture with those of three other girls, noting especially the similarities and differences.

3. Make a comic strip or filmstrip (with U-Film) of an important scene in the book involving two people, such as Margaret's trip with her grandmother or her talk with Laura Danker. Then, with a friend, record on a cassette the dialogue that accompanies the pictures. Use the strip to introduce the book to students who have not read it.

Creative Dramatics

1. Improvise a meeting of the PTS Club. The student who portrays Nancy is responsible for the agenda of the meeting; the others should follow her suggestions just as the members of the club would have done.

2. Act out Norman Fishbein's party and Mrs. Fishbein's reaction to the boys' behavior.

3. Prepare a monologue on one part of the book. Do not memorize the section, but tell it in your own words as if you were Margaret.

Composing

1. Write five entries in a diary Margaret might have kept for five days *after* the book ends.
2. Write a short report comparing the Jewish and Christian religions. Be sure to include the differences in the services, the holidays, and the beliefs.
3. Write a story about something that you looked forward to, something that you anticipated for a long time. Tell exactly how you felt when the moment finally arrived.
4. Make a list of desirable characteristics of boys. Rank these qualities from one to ten. Compare your list with those of your classmates and perhaps make a class tally. (Boys who read the book can make a list for girls.)
5. Write a letter that Margaret might have written to her grandmother at the end of the book.

Instructional Resources

Teaching Guide—Charles F. Reasoner, "Are You There God? It's Me, Margaret," *When Children Read* (New York: Dell Publishing Co., 1975), pp. 201-10.

Sounder

By William H. Armstrong. (New York: Harper & Row, Publishers, 1969, 116 pp. Available in paperback from Harper & Row.)

Summary

Sounder, a coon dog with a magnificent voice, belongs to a poor black family living in the rural South during the Depression. During a bleak winter, the father is arrested for stealing a ham for his family and Sounder is shot. For months, the oldest son hopes futilely for the dog's return while helping his mother cope with the problems of survival. When Sounder finally appears, crippled and silent, the boy's search turns to his father, whose existence in prison work camps remains uncertain. Finally the father returns, but both he and the dog die the following winter, leaving the boy sad, but proud and hopeful of a better life through education. Themes: courage, perseverance, love, loneliness.

Appraisal

Partly because of the excellent motion picture based on the novel, *Sounder* has become one of the most popular books written in recent years. Its beautiful language, its bond between theme and setting, its timeless values, and its powerful story of human courage and endurance are among the book's impressive strengths. Appropriate for students in grades six through eight, *Sounder* won the Newbery Medal for 1970. (It should be noted that the book has been criticized by some, who feel that the characters' acceptance of their fate unfairly stereotypes blacks.)

Reading Considerations

The simplicity of its style helps to bring *Sounder* within reach of many upper-grade readers. Among the more important and possibly challenging words are *addled* (pp. 9, 32, 49, 62, 95, 103), *plaintive* (27), *skittish* (38), *visualize* (45), *compulsion* (84), *fruitless* (85), *askew* (107), and *resolved* (108).

Initiating Activities

1. Read the story of Joseph in the Bible (Genesis 37). Do you think it is a good story? Why or why not? What kind of people do you think would especially like the story? Discuss these questions within your class or group.
2. Try to experience what it is like to be poor. With your parents' permission, live for one day on the food the poor are often restricted to: one or two cold biscuits, corn or liver mush, perhaps a can of milk. Write a paragraph about your reactions to this experience.[1]

Discussion Questions

1. Why is life so harsh for the family? What are some of the ways the mother and father provide for the family?
2. What does the boy discover when he wakes up in the morning? Why is he surprised? Why does his mother frequently hum? Why is she humming this particular morning?
3. "'Stick out your hand, boy,' ordered the second man. The boy started to raise his hands, but the man was already reaching over the stove, snapping handcuffs on the outstretched wrists of his father" (pp. 21-22). What does this scene suggest about how whites treated blacks in this time and place?
*4. On page 30, the narrator says that the boy had "never seen a human animal, like Sounder, dead." What does he mean by "human animal"? Why does the boy keep Sounder's ear?
*5. Why did the father steal the ham? Is stealing ever justified?
6. At the end of Chapter 3, why is the mother "sorry she had asked [the question about the dog's tin plate] and would like to take it back"?

---

[1] Note to the teacher: Obviously, this activity would have to be handled with care and sensitivity if it were used.

*7. Describe the boy's father and the relationship between the two.

8. How does the boy distinguish between house windows and cabin windows? What does the boy mean by the statement "Cabin quiet was long and sad" (p. 51)?

9. Have you ever lost something so important to you that you refused to stop looking for it? Why does the mother say, "Some people is born to keep. Some is born to lose. We was born to lose, I reckon"?

*10. Why does the mother tell the boy to "act perkish" when he delivers the cake? Why is the boy fearful of the town? How does he react to the red-faced man? Have you ever felt such uncontrolled hatred? Do you think the boy's hatred (or any hatred like his) is ever justified?

*11. In what condition does Sounder return? Why does he no longer bark? How do the mother's feelings toward the dog change?

*12. After Sounder's return, "the long days and months and seasons built a powerful restlessness into the boy." What kind of restlessness and yearning is this? Why does the boy's desire to see his father increase as he grows older?

13. Why does the boy like the Bible stories so well?

*14. How does the boy react to cruelty by white men? Why does he think about revenge so vividly? Why doesn't he act out his feelings? Is he a coward? Why or why not?

*15. Why does the boy want to tell the teacher about his life? Why does the boy's mother agree to let him attend school? Does the boy's intense desire to go to school seem strange to you? Why or why not?

*16. In what dramatic way does Sounder greet his returning master? How are they now alike—in ways other than the physical?

*17. In Chapter 7 (p. 95), the teacher tells the boy, "It's hard to reset a plant if it's wilted too much; the life has gone out of it." Considering the tragedies experienced by the boy, what do you think keeps him from "wilting" too much?

Art and Media

1. Design a collage of "What Is Important to Me" as you think the boy would have designed it. If you wish, also make one from your own personal list of important things.

2. Draw a picture of the family cabin and its surroundings so that you emphasize the idea of loneliness.
3. The mother makes a cake for the boy to take to his father. Using clay or wood or other found objects and materials, make something pretty or useful that the children might have sent to their father to remind him of them and raise his spirits.

Creative Dramatics

1. Act out the scene in Chapter 2 where the sheriff and his deputies arrive and arrest the father, but do it as though it had been the house of a white family. In what ways would it have been similar? Different?
2. Improvise the scene in which the mother returns the ham to the person from whom it was stolen.
3. "But mostly they just talked about heat and cold, and wind and clouds, and what's gonna be done, and time passing." With two other students, act out a conversation between the boy and his parents about the past and future after the father returns home.

Composing

1. In a reference book on dogs, find out about coon hounds. What are they like? What breeds contribute to this mixed breed? What are their strengths, uses, etc.? Write your findings in a report.
2. Do you believe that animals can be "human"? Write a paper about an animal you have known, perhaps a dog or cat, that had "human" qualities.
3. Many people believe that poor families like that one in *Sounder* should be helped by federal, state, and local governments to overcome their poverty. Write an argument agreeing or disagreeing with this opinion.
4. Think about a time in your life when you wanted something very badly, something that was very important to you. Write about this period of wanting and waiting.
5. Write a few pages of a diary or journal that the boy might have kept during his travels in search of his father.

Instructional Resources

Record—*Sounder,* Miller-Brody Productions (7-NAR 3018), 33 rpm, $6.95.
Cassette—*Sounder,* Miller-Brody Productions (7-NAC 3018), $7.95.
Feature Film—*Sounder*, 20th Century-Fox, 1972, 105 minutes, color; distributed by Films Inc., $250 vs. 65% of take (rental). Directed by Martin Ritter.
Teaching Kit—*Sounder*, Scholastic Book Services (4926); includes eight-page teaching guide, spirit masters, photographs, all emphasizing setting.

Appendix:
Publishers of Instructional Resources

Angel Records, orders to: Capitol Records, Inc., 1290 Avenue of the Americas, New York, New York 10019.

Caedmon Records, 505 Eighth Avenue, New York, New York 10018.

Contemporary Films/McGraw Hill Films, orders to: 330 West 42 Street, New York, New York 10036.

Cornell University Film Center, Ithaca, New York 14850.

Dell Publishing Company, 1 Dag Hammarskjold Plaza, New York, New York 10017.

Films Inc., 1144 Wilmette Avenue, Wilmette, Illinois 60091.

Harper & Row, Publishers, Inc., 10 East 53 Street, New York, New York 10022.

Holt, Rinehart and Winston, 383 Madison Avenue, New York, New York 10017.

Hudson Photographic Industries, Inc., Educational/Industrial Products Division, Irvington-on-Hudson, New York 10533.

Learning Arts, P.O. Box 917, Wichita, Kansas 67201.

Miller-Brody Productions, Inc., 342 Madison Avenue, New York, New York 10017.

National Geographic Society, 17 and M Streets N.W., Washington, D.C. 20036.

Scholastic Book Services, Division of Scholastic Magazines, Inc., orders to: 906 Sylvan Avenue, Englewood Cliffs, New Jersey 07632.

Society for Visual Education, Inc., 1345 Diversey Parkway, Chicago, Illinois 60614.

Universal/16 United World Films, 445 Park Avenue, New York, New York 10022; 2001 South Vermont Avenue, Los Angeles, California 90001.

University of Iowa Media Library, C-5 East Hall, Iowa City, Iowa
   52242.

University of Nebraska Press, 901 North 17 Street, Lincoln,
   Nebraska 68588.

Weston Woods Studios, Weston, Connecticut 06880.